A LITTLE BIT

OF

TAROT

A LITTLE BIT

OF

TAROT

AN INTRODUCTION TO
READING TAROT

CASSANDRA EASON

STERLING ETHOS
New York

STERLING ETHOS
New York

An Imprint of Sterling Publishing
1166 Avenue of the Americas
New York, NY 10036

ISBN 978-1-4549-1304-7

Distributed in Canada by Sterling Publishing
% Canadian Manda Group, 664 Annette Street
Toronto, Ontario, Canada M6S 2C8
Distributed in the United Kingdom by GMC Distribution Services
Castle Place, 166 High Street, Lewes, East Sussex, England BN7 1XU
Distributed in Australia by Capricorn Link (Australia) Pty. Ltd.
P.O. Box 704, Windsor, NSW 2756, Australia

For information about custom editions, special sales, and premium
and corporate purchases, please contact Sterling Special Sales
at 800-805-5489 or specialsales@sterlingpublishing.com.

Manufactured in the United States of America

8 10 9 7

www.sterlingpublishing.com

CONTENTS

INTRODUCTION: UNDERSTANDING AND ENJOYING THE TAROT

Tarot card reading is the simplest and one of the most effective methods of discovering your potential future paths, as well as the opportunities and challenges for those for whom you read the cards.

In fact, even if you have never used a tarot pack before, from day one you can understand the significance of the cards you have selected by looking at the pictures, relaxing, and letting them guide you to their message.

Indeed, when I taught tarot classes at my local college the very best readings were those done before the students had studied a single card meaning. That was because the students really looked at what the pictures were saying, and not at what they thought they ought to say according to set meanings. They also listened to the person for whom they were reading and tuned in intuitively.

There are seventy-eight cards in a tarot pack, divided into twenty-two Major cards that speak of major events, significant landmarks, the self, and significant others in the questioner's life, and fifty-six Minor cards, which consist of four different suits.

These fifty-six cards offer more information about the influence on our lives of those around us, the context of the questions we are asking, and sometimes the constraints within which we make our decisions.

These suits begin with an ace (or one) and go to ten, or completion. Included in the suits are sixteen court cards: pages or princesses, princes or knights, queens and kings. These refer to people in your life—past, present, or future—or strengths and qualities you can develop.

I will explain each card in greater detail in the following chapters.

DEVELOPING A TAROT READING SYSTEM THAT IS RIGHT FOR YOU

As you gain confidence, you will create your own system of reading the cards. Books offer suggestions on layouts and the way to carry out a reading, as well as basic meanings of individual cards; but these are a basic template for you to make card reading your own.

This book is filled with ideas I have found useful in my more than forty years of giving readings, teaching, and writing—and above all constantly revising my ideas and practices. However, you will discover what works for you best by also experimenting with different ways of choosing cards and getting others to select them.

Like driving a car, at first you are aware of the different processes; but gradually everything becomes automatic and you focus on the route and scenery, as well as the enjoyable company of your passengers. This is the same with the tarot.

Throughout this book are different layouts—you will develop favorites, but more important, you will adapt them or even devise your own layouts that make sense for you.

Tarot reading is a matter of trusting yourself and what you *feel* as opposed to what you *think* or try to deduce from the cards. Because once analysis kicks in, the psychic self that has access to what is forming ahead gets drowned out.

HOW TAROT READING ACTUALLY WORKS

You or the person for whom you are reading will always select from the pack, seemingly at random, the relevant cards to answer a question through a psychic process called psychokinesis.

Psychokinesis is the power that automatically guided cave-dwelling hunters to where the animals were and at the same time *drew* creatures to the hunting grounds. Dowsing, in which people find oil, water, minerals, or missing objects, and even enemy submarines on a map, using rods or a pendulum, is also psychokinesis.

We are all psychic, but after childhood our powers can be overridden by logic and doubts. Yet you do instinctively *know* things without having access to relevant information. Parents have an automatic radar that is activated when children are in danger or distress, even when far away from their kids; lots of adults pick up the phone to dial at the same time as a mom, dad, brother, or sister is phoning them, especially if something is wrong.

Another psychic power, called clairvoyance, comes to the fore as the card pictures trigger images in your mind; you will also access your innate clairaudience when you hear in your mind words or phrases either from your own inner wise self or from your angels and guides that give you information via the cards. You will also be affected by claircognizance, that sense of *knowing* something that is subsequently proven right, without being aware of how you know it. These are the tools you use spontaneously when reading cards. Indeed, the more you read the tarot, the more you activate your psychic gifts in your everyday life.

CHOOSING THE RIGHT PACK

Select a highly illustrated pack, for example, the Rider Waite, upon which the majority of modern packs are based. Some of my favorites are the Universal Waite, the Druidcraft Tarot, the Celtic Tarot, the Mythic Tarot, or the Morgan Greer pack. These packs are ideal for learning because every card, not just the first twenty-two Major cards, has a picture to guide you.

THE PICTURES TRIGGER OUR OWN INNER CLAIRVOYANT OR PSYCHIC IMAGERY SYSTEM

Despite superstition, it is not at all unlucky to buy your own cards, and if a friend or partner wants to give you your first pack, you can suggest you pick it together and make a day of it (better still, buy two packs—one for each of you—and learn together).

Even if you are choosing packs alone, make this a fun day so your pack begins its relationship with you with happiness. If selecting via the Internet, have your little celebration when they arrive.

Have a quick look through this book before you look through your pack so that you can familiarize yourself with the basic names of the individual cards. Select a pack with the standard seventy-eight cards, which are instantly recognizable from the names in the book. Occasionally packs will use obscure names for individual cards or introduce complex concepts such as astrology or Egyptian mythology, so keep this in mind as you inspect them.

Once you become more adept you may find another pack that works better. I often work with two or more different packs at the same time because if a client picks the same card from more than one pack then you can be sure it is of significance.

If at all possible, buy tarot packs from a new age store or bookshop where there are different packs you can see and handle. If buying off the Internet, choose a site where you can see the Minor as well as the Major cards or trawl the Internet for sites that describe individual card sets in detail and illustrate the key ones on the site.

When you reach home, take the cards out of the box, place the face-down pack on the table, and pass your hand over them as if pushing away smoke, palm flat and facing down. Move your hand over the cards and around them, about an inch above the pack, and say, "I ask the wise angels to guide me always to use this pack for the greatest good to others and with wisdom and compassion."

You can do this before a reading if you are in a hurry, and you can refresh the energies after a reading in the same way. I have also provided a longer dedication and empowerment at the end of this introduction.

YOUR FIRST READING

Here are a few things to keep in mind as you do your first reading.

Ask a question that matters, then shuffle or mix the pack face-down and place the cards again face-down in a single pile, so you can't see the pictures. Hold the pack in the hand that feels most comfortable and, without thinking, allow your hand to select one, two, or three cards—whichever feels right—and set each of these cards in a left-to-right row or top-to-bottom column.

If you prefer, set the cards in a face-down circle and allow your hand (again, whichever one feels right), from about an inch above the pack, to be drawn to the right number of cards. On the whole it seems more natural to choose cards with the hand you write with. In this book I have suggested a number of specific ways of spreading the cards you select, but for more general life issues or a life review, you may find it useful not to assign set position meanings but to allow the cards to build up a story one by one (more on this later). For this first reading, if you are using three cards, leave them face-down and choose one that you feel instinctively is the key.

Turn the first card over and look at it, not attempting to analyze it or to fit it in with the question you asked, but simply memorizing the details of the card. Now put down the card, close your eyes, and see the card in your mind as though set on a blue or white screen, so tapping into your clairvoyant vision. If you cannot see the card in your mind, open your eyes and stare at the card again until you can picture every detail, and then close your eyes and let the card form in your mind.

At this stage, let the inner card become three-dimensional and follow the river or go into the depicted house with the family outside. Enjoy the sensation, but do not force anything and just let a story or idea emerge. Open your eyes once more, pick up a pen, and let your hand write words or even scribble images totally spontaneously. Do not read what you have written until you have completed choosing, memorizing, and writing all the cards. Read what you have written and you will find you have answered the question. You could keep a special tarot diary for your findings.

Your Daily Tarot Card

Card readings for yourself help you to monitor your life path and anticipate opportunities and pitfalls ahead of the crowd.

Each morning pick a card from the face-down pack (shuffle the cards if you wish). Look at the picture and it will give clues to the day ahead and useful strategies. Note this down in a daily journal as well as anything that immediately springs to mind as images, words, or impressions and feelings. If the same card appears for several days or on a specific day of the week, you know that it represents an issue that needs resolving or maximizing.

For example, if you picked the Chariot with the young charioteer steering his two horses, you would know that it was a day for action and change. Because he is controlling the direction of the chariot, maybe it is time for you to take charge of a situation or change direction and spread your wings.

Empowering Your Tarot Cards

Rather than keeping your cards in the box, buy a large fabric wallet or drawstring bag. Some practitioners wrap the pack in white silk or natural fabric within the bag.

If you read with good intentions, only good will emerge from your readings and this in and of itself offers inbuilt protection.

There are two angels who are dedicated to clairvoyants, Raziel and Nithaiah, and you can call on them for protection before doing a reading, as well as afterward, and as you learn, ask them to bless and protect your tarot work and keep you safe from all harm.

Raziel, archangel of spiritual work, has swirling robes with deep green flares in his halo.

The silvery Nithaiah is the angel of poets as well as prophecy and carries a silver scroll.

Light two white candles side by side, the larger one for Raziel and the smaller for Nithaiah (light the smaller from the larger), and say,

"I ask wise Raziel and gentle Nithaiah to make my cards always an instrument of wisdom and compassion. I request they will guide me always to use this pack for the greatest good of others and will keep away from me and those for whom I read all harm, malice, and darkness."

Set the cards in a clockwise circle, in the order they naturally emerge, pictures uppermost, and let the light shine on them.

Leave the candles to burn through.

Before a reading, light the two candles, blow softly three times into each flame, and, after blowing, ask Raziel in the first larger candle and Nithaiah in the other that they will bless and protect you and any person you are reading for, and leave the candles on a side table.

After the reading, thank the two angels for their protection and blow out the two candles, sending the light to whoever needs it (not forgetting yourself).

You can also leave the cards in the face-down pile open on the night of the full moon on an indoor window ledge to fill them with power.

In the first chapter we will begin to learn the card meanings and simple layouts. But remember, in essence, the introduction actually teaches you all you need to know for intuitive readings. Many excellent tarot readers work instinctively without learning any set meanings, adding and turning over as many cards they feel are needed and reading the pictures.

1

THE FIRST TWELVE MAJOR TWENTY-TWO CARDS

A STANDARD TAROT PACK HAS TWENTY-TWO MAJOR Arcana cards (*Arcana* means "hidden wisdom," as in what you will uncover during your readings).

STARTING A TAROT JOURNAL

One suggestion as you begin your tarot practice is to create a journal that will allow you to focus your thoughts.

Use a plain-paged cloth or leather-bound book, the kind that is a binder so you can add or remove pages. As you write in this book, it will reflect your unfolding tarot journey.

Start a page for each card. Before reading the meaning of each card as described on the following pages, hold the card in the hand you do not write with and look at the picture. Write in your journal what you instinctively feel about the card and the ideas it suggests to you. You may be surprised how close to the conventional meaning you are when you read it afterward.

If a card especially interests you, create its story—why and where; for example, the little boy was riding his white horse in the Sun card and who he was. Add to the basic card meanings every time the card appears in a reading and you have a new insight. Note also any special readings with dates so you can track how the predictions unfold in your life or in those of the people for whom you read.

Draw any new spreads you learn and how you have adapted them with position meanings to suit you if they do not feel quite right.

Record your card of the day so you can see any sequences and patterns, perhaps if a particular card regularly turns up on a certain day when a difficult relative visits or you have to cover a shift you do not enjoy.

THE MAJOR CARDS

The Major cards will be numbered either zero to twenty-one or one to twenty-two. The order of cards will be the same regardless of the pack you use, with the exception of Strength and Justice, which are interchangeable as numbers eight and eleven.

The Fool, the Intuition Card

The Fool is the ultimate new beginning card and says that anything is possible.

The Fool represents an inner change, usually as a response to an unexpected opportunity or a desire to find or rediscover your own identity.

If that unexpected opportunity hasn't yet turned up, it will very soon. Instead of saying, "I couldn't possibly," the Fool says, "What's to stop you?"

Trust your intuition, take that leap into the dark, and, whatever you do, don't look down as you jump.

IN THE EVERYDAY WORLD

The Fool talks about lightening up, being spontaneous, going on a spur-of-the-moment excursion, or repainting the living room buttercup yellow.

The Fool's only drawback is he does act impulsively and immaturely.

1 The Magician or Juggler, the Making Things Happen Card

The Magician signifies creativity, ingenuity, and the ability and need to think outside the box.

The card is a good omen for setting up or running your own business, especially in a creative field. Now is the time and chance to put plans into action and test your creations in the marketplace, even if you start from small beginnings.

The Magician can indicate a powerful, charismatic personality who will open doors for you. You may be attracted to this person and enjoy a passionate, emotionally charged relationship.

The Magician indicates a good time for speculation and investments, networking, media, and interviews of all kinds. Any form of communication is favored, whether in person, in writing, or by e-mail or phone. Ask and your demands will be met.

The only downside is you can get the occasional conman and illusionist Magician.

2 The High Priestess or Popess, the Doing Your Own Thing Card

This is about the real you, whatever age you are.

The High Priestess is the sister and alter ego of the motherly and very caring Empress. She tells us to ask ourselves what we really want from our lives and, even if we are in a close relationship or caring for a family, to make time for quiet periods to reconnect with the inner self and private dreams.

Being alone is not the same as being lonely, so learn to value your own company. You have healing powers.

IN THE EVERYDAY WORLD

The High Priestess may appear when there is a lot of gossip or pettiness in your immediate work or home circle and the card says you should rise above it. Don't be tempted to take sides or act as a peacemaker, but make sure you do not reveal confidences even for the best motives.

Her downside is she can take life too seriously and lack tolerance for others' weakness.

3 The Empress, the Nurturing Others Card

The Empress is the Mother Earth card. For men and women of childbearing years, this is the ultimate pregnancy and birth card for you or a partner, especially if you are worried about fertility.

You are central to the happiness and well-being of others with family and friends and can work successfully in a career in which you care for others. She promises the fruition of projects and family joy.

IN THE EVERYDAY WORLD

Someone close needs extra tender loving care and you may need to bring the family together. Time with your own mother or grand-mother would be fruitful, especially if there has been some coldness.

Her downside is on becoming a martyr or overinvolved in the lives of others and being possessive or living through them.

4 The Emperor, the Power and Achievement Card

The Emperor is the card of fatherhood, determination, and earthly success. He represents the father and authority role. For women as well as men, he can signify an older relative who influences them, a powerful and very successful love partner (or potentially so if young), or an authority figure of either sex who is closely involved with your world.

For both sexes, the message is that you can gain promotion or achieve your goals if you do not hold back and you act more assertively than usual.

IN THE EVERYDAY WORLD

You may need to be more forceful than usual to avoid being overlooked or not given due credit, and you should make an all-or-nothing effort. You may need to spend more time with a father, grandfather, or older male relative, or if you have children you should take a stand over some aspect of their behavior.

The downside of the Emperor is he can be strongly critical and hard to please. You should not be bullied, whether this is your partner, a relative of either sex, or a boss.

5 The Hierophant or Pope, the Traditional Path Card

The Hierophant is brother and alter ego of the Emperor and is a source of wisdom, spiritual and traditional knowledge, and experience rather than authority and material success.

If you are considering a course of study or training that may seem long and difficult, this will lead to a more fulfilling career or lifestyle. He also favors learning and practicing teaching, spirituality, or psychic development.

As a person in your life, he signifies a wise teacher or counselor, whether a friend, family member, or spiritual or professional adviser, and he may indicate love with a spiritually focused person.

The Hierophant indicates we shouldn't take a shortcut or find a quick-fix solution, but that we need to fill in the forms, study the small print, and go through official channels for now.

Don't let past failures stop you from believing in yourself.

On the downside, he can be narrow-minded and prejudiced. The inner Hierophant represents old prohibitive voices from the past—he's the traffic warden in our head—making us overcautious.

6 The Lovers, the Love and Relationships Card

The Lovers card is about love and can indicate a twin soul if you are in a committed relationship or have met someone who feels special and as if you have known him or her all your life.

It is an assurance that love in an existing relationship will be real and lasting.

The card can indicate choices between two people in love and the answer is to pick the person who stirs your heart, even if that means leaving security.

If you are unattached, love is coming soon.

The Lovers card appears when a relationship needs input or a little extra attention, or if you have reached a change point and need to rekindle the connection and explore new directions together. It can also say that you are ready for the next stage in a relationship, whether commitment or the consummation of love.

The downside is the temptation to throw away constant love for a few hours' excitement or a wild affair.

7 The Chariot, the Choosing Your Own Route Card

The Chariot is the card of action that indicates change and excitement. Whatever your age or stage of life, this is a card of triumph and going forward, whether moving house, traveling, or making a major or minor life shift in career and lifestyle, or maybe even taking a more adventurous holiday than usual.

The key to this card is who steers the chariot—and so determines the direction—and for true happiness that must be you, however much you want to please others.

Clear the clutter of your life, bad habits, outgrown activities, even people, focusing on fitness and health and doing things you have always postponed for later. It can also herald an unexpected travel opportunity.

The downside is constantly changing the external circumstances when the problem or restlessness is within you.

8 (or 11) Strength, the Overcoming Obstacles Card

Strength is a good card for reassuring you that you will have the ability to achieve your goal and overcome obstacles if you persevere.

It also refers to your untapped strengths and talents and says that you have great resources to win, though it may be a hard and uphill task, especially if you are undertaking a long-term project. Strength can also refer to a strong but gentle person on whom you can rely and it indicates that old trusted friends will prove more loyal than exciting new ones who promise the moon.

IN THE EVERYDAY WORLD

You may need to be patient and persevere with difficult people and situations; don't let anyone dissuade you from a course of action you feel is right. Don't waste your strength trying to win round someone stubborn, as that person will never see your point of view.

The only drawback of Strength is if you are pouring your efforts into a lost cause.

9 | The Hermit, the Following Your Own Principle Card

The Hermit counsels following your own path and principles. It can appear when you feel lost, but it says you are not lost at all but you just need the space and time to allow all the factors to emerge. Postpone a major decision for now, even if you are being pressured to make up your mind.

If someone close refuses to stop some destructive behavior and blames you for the situation, refuse to accept guilt or blame and step back.

The Hermit can also be a wise older person who has time to listen and will not judge you.

IN THE EVERYDAY WORLD

You may be acting as peacemaker between warring factions and find both sides blame you—step back. Quarreling, especially within a family, may cease if there is no audience.

The only drawbacks of the Hermit are allowing inertia to take over and relying too much on the wisdom and expertise of others.

10 | The Wheel of Fortune, the Making Your Own Fortune Card

The Wheel of Fortune usually appears after a run of bad luck or opportunities that have not materialized, and it heralds an upturn in fortunes, especially financial.

Though the card does indicate unexpected good luck, in the end you make your own fortune, so use both lucky breaks and reversals to shape your future destiny.

You may benefit from a lucky break that involves risking temporary security. Take a chance.

IN THE EVERYDAY WORLD

The Wheel of Fortune indicates a good time to enter a competition or have a small bet on the lottery. You may get some unexpected money or a chance for some extra short-term work connected with an interest or talent—this will bring good returns.

The only downside to the Wheel is if you wait for the perfect opportunity or the ideal circumstances to launch yourself into life.

(or 8) Justice, the Getting What You Are Owed Card

Justice is about fairness in life and often appears when you are entangled in a legal matter, a compensation issue, or maybe a divorce or a dispute with an official body such as the tax authorities or an education official. Justice says persist; do not be intimidated by the big boys and girls, and you will win.

Justice can also turn up when you are being exploited by family, intimidated by neighbors or an employer, or doing more than your fair share of work owing to lazy, dishonest, or incompetent colleagues. Keep notes and dates, and if in a workplace dispute, go through official channels of protest. It could be that some deal, offer, or person who is helping with your work or financial affairs may be corrupt—you probably sensed this anyway.

You may need to weigh both sides of an argument before making a decision; also remain impartial and don't play favorites with the family or take the side of one friend against another.

The negative aspect of Justice is holding on to past injustices that can't be resolved.

12 The Hanged Man, the Letting Go Card

In spite of the somewhat spooky name, the Hanged Man talks of letting go of fears and all the restrictions that keep us from surrendering ourselves wholeheartedly to life—or to love.

IN THE EVERYDAY WORLD

Let go of destructive relationships, draining careers, and emotional vampires, when you feel you cannot survive without them or are responsible for their well-being. If you are struggling to quit bad habits, phobias, or addictions, take it a day at a time and you will be free sooner than you think.

The only downside of the Hanged Man is if you sacrifice yourself for an unworthy cause or keep giving an unreliable or unworthy person chance after chance.

A THREE-OR FOUR-CARD READING USING THE FIRST TWELVE MAJOR CARDS: THE MAKING CHANGES SPREAD

This is an excellent basic spread you can do with the entire seventy-eight-card pack or the whole Major Arcana. But for now we are going to use the first twelve cards.

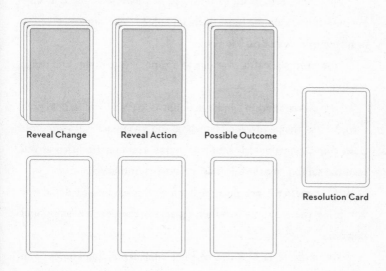

Reveal Change   Reveal Action   Possible Outcome

Resolution Card

Formulate a question concerning a change you need or would like to make. This may reveal unexpected undercurrents affecting actions.

Take the first twelve cards, shuffle or mix them, and either return them to the pile face-down or place them in a face-down circle.

Let your hand guide you to the first card to reveal what you need to leave behind or change. Set this card in the far left Reveal Change Position, but do not turn it over yet.

Pick a second card and set it in the Reveal Action Position to represent the action you need to take now or helpful factors that will move the matter forward. Again, do not turn it over.

Finally, select a third card and set it in the Possible Outcome Position to indicate the most likely outcome of the suggested action or influence. Do not turn it over.

Now turn the cards over one at a time, left to right, and begin reading.

Don't force anything and if in doubt as to significance, hold each card, look at the picture, and let words and images as well as impressions come spontaneously into your mind. You may find that as you read the subsequent cards it is as if a story is unfolding.

If the matter is not clear, pick a fourth resolution card and this will bring the messages together, especially the possible action and outcome.

You will see factors you had not considered, sometimes from years back, clouding the present and future.

A Real-Life Reading

This was a reading when four of the first twelve cards did turn up from a full Major Arcana reading in the Making Changes spread.

Anna is twenty and shares an apartment with her best friend, Lizzie. Anna's boyfriend, Steve, comes to stay every weekend and Anna finds herself dashing around and clearing up before he comes, as Lizzie lets the place become a wreck. What is more, though, Steve always brings a bottle of wine, but Anna ends up buying all the food for the three of them, as she often does during the week because Lizzie is always broke (though she has a good job). When they go out for a meal, Anna pays and Lizzie invariably joins the couple without being asked.

But when Anna half jokingly suggests the others contribute to a particularly expensive dinner when Lizzie and Steve picked absolutely everything from the à la carte menu, Lizzie just laughs and tells Steve that Anna is mean with money.

Anna's father left home to live with another woman when Anna was small, and one of the arguments that Anna can remember was her father constantly accusing her mother of nagging him about money and about his making a mess.

Anna's question was "Am I being mean?"

CARD ONE: The Empress for the Change Position: The Empress card reinforces the mothering role Anna is being forced into by people quite capable of looking after and paying for themselves, but the change she is seeking is a little more complex. Does Anna actually want to change this dependency pattern, and if not, why not?

Anna realized as we talked that she is acting out her father's accusations against her mother (actually not true, as her father was a gambler and there was never enough money, and when he came home drunk, he would throw everything on the floor and often be sick).

So Anna needs to change not her behavior but her perception of the current situation through the eyes of the past.

CARD TWO: The Reveal Action: The Chariot says that it's clearly time for a change and that Anna must initiate the changes she wants and steer the Chariot. How? She realized if she went to her boyfriend's apartment on the other side of the city over the weekend, she and her boyfriend could go out for meals without Lizzie trailing along, itself a cause of irritation to Anna because Lizzie flirted with Steve. This would lift from Anna the onus and expense of catering for three, as well as the need to clean up before Steve arrived.

What is more, Anna needs to decide whether to stop cleaning up her roommate's mess and ignore it, or impose sanctions like refusing to cook for her roommate.

CARD THREE: The Possible Outcome: The Lovers card refers not only to Anna's relationship with her boyfriend but also with her roommate. By playing out an old scenario and desperately trying not to repeat what she saw as her mother's mistakes, Anna is not relating to Steve and Lizzie as they are or their selfish behavior as it is. Steve may simply be thoughtless, for until very recently he was living at home with his mother, and Anna may find that when she tries to initiate changes, Steve may go along with them.

When Anna views her roommate as an individual, and not someone whom she has to "mother," she may realize that, in fact, she no longer wishes to live with her; or she can at least can be sufficiently detached to counter Lizzie's quite unfair accusation of meanness with a few justified barbs of her own.

Even more important, she can get to know her boyfriend without interference so she can decide if he really is the one for her.

Because she wanted further clarification, Anna picked a fourth card, which was Justice.

Since the Justice card can refer to divorces, and her father left her mother, the Resolution card casts up Anna's unrecognized fears that if she makes a fuss, Steve will leave her just as her father left her mother. Deep down, Anna told me she feels she was responsible for her parents' unhappiness. It isn't logical, but it is very understandable. So Anna is trying, in her adult life, to make up for a guilt she picked up in childhood.

It's not only mothers who end up servicing others, and I have come across many cases similar to Anna's in which a perfectly competent, successful young woman feels unable to assert herself in the field of personal relationships.

2

THE FINAL TEN MAJOR CARDS

L OOK AT EACH CARD BEFORE STUDYING THE
meaning and write in your journal what you see, hear, and
feel. Remember that every card has positive and challenging
meanings, according to how the card fits with others in a spread—and,
most important, what you feel.

 Death, the Natural Change Card

**There is absolutely no way that turning up the death card means
that you or anyone else close to you are going to die.**

The Death card usually represents a door you need to close on a
situation or relationship that is holding you back from finding happiness, a loss that will be painful but will free you. If you do not close
that door, the new beginnings will not develop.

Sometimes it's time to say "no" once and for all to family members, work colleagues, or an employer who is pressuring you into something you're not happy with. It can also occur if you are feeling sad about an ending and scared of being alone. Don't rush headlong into the next stage or relationship until you are ready.

The only negative aspect of this card is if you feel so guilty about how a person or workplace you need to leave will manage, then you can't move forward.

14 Temperance, the Finding the Balance Card

Temperance is the good fairy of the pack, the card of balance and harmony, both within you and around you.

Health-wise, it talks about the return or continuation of good health; any medical treatment or healing will bring better results than hoped for. In any situation, steer a middle course and avoid excesses. Peacemaking and negotiation in a job situation or family gathering are the way forward.

Temperance is also the card of accepting what can't be changed and letting the old resentments go.

Good for tackling tricky or sensitive issues and for communicating with difficult people or between generations, also for dieting or giving up any addiction or excess even if you've failed in the past. Don't be tempted to act as a messenger of bad news or be tempted by the misconduct of another.

The negative side of Temperance is keeping the peace at all costs. That can have a very high price, especially in terms of your own peace of mind.

15 The Devil, the Pressure-Cooker Card

This card has nothing to do with black magic or evil but talks about all the stored accumulated power you have that right now you are not using, or it speaks to justifiable resentments you have not expressed that are building up inside. You need to set boundaries on what you will tolerate.

IN THE EVERYDAY WORLD

If people are being unfair or unreasonable right now in any aspect of your life, say so. You will be releasing suppressed energy into your life (bad for your health and well-being), which, at the moment, is being used to keep the lid on justifiable reactions to unfair treatment.

The only negative aspect of the Devil is if you wait too long to release the pressure and end up being angry at the wrong person or becoming depressed.

16 The Tower of Liberation, the Rebuilding Better than Before Card

The Tower, traditionally called the Tower of Destruction, is in fact a sign of freedom from constraints in your life. It refers to an event that is happening at the time of the reading or an event you know is necessary to clear stagnation, inertia, and restrictions.

The card can represent the clearing of actual obstacles in your path that have been holding you back from fulfilling your potential or happiness. Yes, there will be disruption, but it will give you a far more open fulfilling future and even a new lifestyle.

IN THE EVERYDAY WORLD

The Tower can indicate that a temporary cash flow or debt problem may soon be eased by an unexpected opportunity to make some money or by freeing up your resources; if you have been feeling trapped by your work situation or have been confined at home or in a bad relationship, there will be a significant breakthrough—especially if you reach out to seek the support you need.

The only negative aspect of the Tower is not learning from the mistakes and building an identical tower in another place—and wondering why it falls down again.

17 The Star, the Realistic Dreams Coming True Card

Whatever your dream, however unlikely, it can come true if you work toward it and maybe in ways beyond your imagination, for this is the card of fame as well as fortune.

The time is now to reach for your perhaps unexpressed or even acknowledged dreams that will transform your life and give it meaning.

The Star, like the Wheel of Fortune, is also a good-luck card and indicates that the tide of better fortune is turning in your favor.

IN THE EVERYDAY WORLD

You may suddenly find yourself in the limelight and you will shine, so be confident. It's a good time to enter competitions or games of chance; you may also gain a new friend or secret admirer or experience a revival in your social life.

The only negative aspect of the Star is if your idea of perfection is so high you never consider yourself good enough to test your talents in the wider world.

18 The Moon, the Moving to the Next Phase of Your Life Card

The Moon says beware the easy option, the shortcut. Whether it's financial or a romantic fling, it may have dire consequences; beware illusions and people who promise the moon but are caught in their own fantasy world. Equally, however, for women, the moon heralds a natural move to the next phase of your life and favors all matters concerning children and animals, imaginative enterprises, alternative medicine, spirituality, or clairvoyance.

The Moon is another excellent fertility card, especially if there have been difficulties.

IN THE EVERYDAY WORLD

Every drama king or queen in the world may be off-loading their emotions on you, and emotional pressure's coming from all sides. Be gentle with yourself and don't give way to emotional blackmail.

The downside of the moon is to spend so much time dreaming you never make anything happen in your day-to-day life.

19 The Sun, the Success Card

The Sun promises happiness, fulfillment, and success in the world's terms. It talks about achieving ambitions and making money, but also finding what makes you truly happy. Don't worry about the future—seize the moment and go all out for what you want.

The Sun card also speaks of emerging untapped or undeveloped talents whatever your age or life stage, and it says you can turn interests into a new and lucrative career and push open previously closed doors.

IN THE EVERYDAY WORLD

Anxieties about health will ease and new financial sources emerge. Holidays or working in sunny places may appear—or you may get a chance to work with a partner or close friend on a profitable and high-profile venture in the not-too-distant future.

The only down side of the Sun is overworking to the exclusion of loved ones and leisure—and sometimes even burnout.

20 Judgment, the Rebirth and Regeneration Card

Judgment centers on making your own assessment of a person or situation if conflicting opinions or judgmental people are causing you to doubt yourself—usually because they have a vested interest in keeping control.

It can appear when a course of action has not worked out and you need to start again in a new way or setting. Resolve what can be fixed and let the rest go, whether old guilt or others' unfair criticism of your life.

Don't take what you have been told as fact, especially if the source was gossip or rumor. A legal or official matter, an interview, or forthcoming test or examination will be resolved in your favor. Others may be trying to steal your ideas, so make sure you get the credit.

The downside of Judgment is falling for those who play favorites; take yourself out of the outworn power games and give up trying to please.

21 The World, the Wishes Fulfilled Card

The World is the card of anything is possible and of expansion in every way, whether in business or trying new interests and social groups. Travel is especially fortunate, particularly long-distance, or making a long-term and long-distance house move. You may have to relocate or look further for the ideal opportunity.

IN THE EVERYDAY WORLD

Everything is coming to fruition. The World suggests an unexpected chance to travel, or if you are in business, to benefit from overseas and Internet connections. Invitations and offers pour in.

The only downside of the World is living the dreams of others and abandoning your own, even with the best of motives.

A THREE-, SIX-, AND NINE-CARD READING

You can use a three-card spread when you are in a hurry or have a specific question to answer, a six-card spread for more detail or a more complex issue, and a full nine-card spread for a matter that is not so clear or may involve a major life change. You also have the option of adding a tenth card at the top if the answer seems unresolved.

Begin with a question, an area of concern, or let the cards unfold their message quite spontaneously.

Shuffle or mix the cards face-down in any way that feels right and divide the cards into three approximately equal face-down packs.

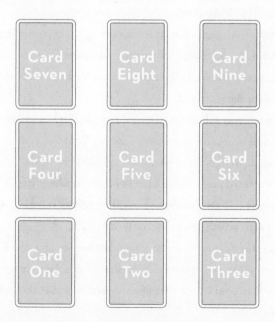

From the pile on the left, pick a card from anywhere in the pile and set card number one in position one (on page 27). From the middle pile in the same way, take card two and from the third pile take card three.

Continue with this sequence, one pile after another, left to right. If you are doing a six- or nine-card sequence, set each card in ascending order in the spread; for six cards, use two rows, and for nine cards, use three rows, always left to right.

Now you have an option. Experiment with both methods to decide which works best for you.

Turn all the cards over, one at a time, bottom to top, left to right, and then read all the cards.

Alternatively, turn the cards over one at a time, again bottom to top, left to right, according to whether it is a three-, six-, or nine-card reading, so the picture is uppermost. Read each card picture before turning over the next card.

The method I describe next and the one that works best for me is to turn all your cards over before reading. That way you may get an overall impression before looking at the individual cards.

Which card seems to hold the key to the reading? Begin reading this key card and then read the cards in the order you dealt them, or choose a card order that instinctively feels right.

Note if any cards naturally fit together (for example, the Emperor and Empress) and whether you immediately associate them with any individuals in your life or that of the questioner. Ask the questioner for associations.

A Real-Life Reading

The following is a real-life nine-card reading using the Major Arcana.

Veronica, a calm, competent woman, went back to work when her daughter was three months old. Veronica has built up a good career in design, but at forty-five, she found herself unexpectedly pregnant and everyone, including her husband, feels she is too old to have another child and that it will hinder her career.

But lately Veronica has come to realize that she isn't enjoying a high-powered life very much and actually would prefer to spend more time at home, working on a part-time freelance basis, as she has many ideas for creative projects connected with children that would fulfill a part of herself she lost after college. Secretly, Veronica is pleased about the baby because she feels she missed out on her first daughter's babyhood and regrets this. Following are the cards that Veronica drew.

KEY CARD: The Devil (actually in the card-one position, but this will not always necessarily be so).

CARD ONE: The Devil: The pregnancy has surfaced a lot of negative feelings, doubts, and regrets about the way Veronica's life has been and she is aware that she has missed so many of her daughter's milestones. Once Veronica expresses these to her husband and family, she will feel so much better, as everyone assumes that because she is so successful she must be blissfully happy with her life—and Veronica has not felt she could say otherwise, until now.

CARD TWO: The Tower of Liberation: Some might see the Tower in the traditional Tower of Destruction sense with the pregnancy threatening Veronica's career. But in fact the new baby is the means of releasing Veronica from a life that she is increasingly finding restrictive. Therefore, it truly is the Tower of Liberation. Being at home could also help Veronica work in a way she finds more creative and less stressful.

CARD THREE: The Star: This card suggests that Veronica has the chance to make her own very realistic dreams come true, starting from where she is and using her experience both professionally and as a mother in her new creations. Of course, they are not the dreams other people might have for her, and they are certainly not the dreams she had ten years ago. But she has fulfilled one side of her life and now wants to enjoy motherhood and creativity.

CARD FOUR: Death: Death marks the ending of a natural stage with Veronica's later-in-life pregnancy. If she goes ahead with her wishes and ignores everyone else she will be giving up a lot materially, but on the other hand, she will be able to develop bonds with her existing daughter and have more time to spend with her husband if both of them are not constantly dashing around. The income aspect is no longer so vital because her husband has a successful business.

CARD FIVE: The High Priestess: Veronica has always prided herself on being an independent woman who has made her own way in the world. But she is constantly stressed from working late, trying to spend quality time with the family (especially her daughter), and juggling everything. When her daughter called Veronica's mother *mom* by mistake, Veronica felt she had sacrificed too much for her luxury lifestyle.

CARD SIX: The Empress: Now Veronica can reclaim the role of mother to both her daughter and her soon-to-be new baby and this is of course a very creative card that promises that Veronica's artistic design work for children will also bear fruit. Veronica feels excited and scared, of course, but alive for the first time in years.

CARD SEVEN: The Hierophant: The Hierophant and the Empress are linked. Veronica is feeling guilty because she is considering turning her back on her hard-won success, and this has not been helped by the scathing comments of successful female colleagues, who think she is selling out.

CARD EIGHT: The Fool: The Fool suggests that ultimately Veronica should follow her own gut feeling, not other people's advice, and that if she wants the baby she should have it.

CARD NINE: The World: This may seem to be a strange card on the surface for a woman who is about to give up work and stay at home, but in fact her horizons will expand as she explores creativity and enjoys family life. Even more significantly, because her husband travels extensively in his business, there are plenty of opportunities for the family to travel together and to live abroad during summer when there is no school. This will enable Veronica to rekindle the relationship with her husband that has suffered because of his frequent absences and her frantic lifestyle.

CARD OF THE DAY

Don't forget to keep picking your single card of the day in the morning and noting it down. You can check the meaning, but first again ask, "What does this card make me feel?" If a particular person or situation triggers the same card week after week, try a three-card reading to see what solutions are cast.

3

THE MEANING
OF THE
FOUR SUITS
AND THE
ACES IN
THE TAROT

ONCE YOU HAVE LEARNED THE TWENTY-TWO Major cards, the rest of the tarot pack falls into a logical pattern. There are two aspects of the next forty cards, the four different suits or kinds of cards, and the numbers one or Ace to ten. The Court cards, Pages to Kings, are in a separate chapter but also follow the basic four-suit meanings.

The suit cards offer more detail about the influence of those around us on our lives and the context and sometimes constraints within which we make our decisions. As I suggested in the introduction, choose a pack with illustrated suit cards, as the pictures trigger our own inner clairvoyant or psychic imagery system.

THE SUITS IN DETAIL

Following is a description of the four suits: pentacles; cups or chalices; wands, rods, or staves; and swords.

Pentacles, Discs, or Coins, the Suit of the Material World; the Practical Approach

Pentacles are the suit of security, stability, and of the practical organization of our daily lives.

Pentacles talk of the home, the family, animals, financial matters, and property—especially land deals and house moves. The latter are generally planned and gradual rather than a sudden uprooting. Pentacles can also refer to dealings with officialdom and financial institutions.

Pentacles advise using common sense, checking facts and figures, as well as a practical, pragmatic approach to problems. Any Pentacles venture will be step-by-step, but have a sure foundation and be assured long-term success.

Patience and persistence are its virtues and a reluctance to consider new approaches or valuing possessions over people are its faults.

Cups or Chalices, the Suit of Water; the Suit of Love and Emotions

Cups or chalices are the suit of love, friendship, fidelity, and all matters connected with the environment, nature, and the seasons.

Cups represent lovers, from a love as yet undiscovered to long-standing partnerships and marriages, choices in love, and the emotional as opposed to practical (Pentacles) aspects of family relationships. They also relate to personal harmony, fertility, psychic abilities, alternative healing, and reconciliation—or if things are not working out, walking away from a destructive or possessive relationship.

They advise following your heart, not logic, and of finding fulfillment with and through other people. Empathy and sympathy are its virtues. Allowing you to become emotionally pressured, codependent, or oversentimental are its faults.

Wands, Rods, or Staves, the Suit of Fire; the World of Inspiration and Creativity

Wands are the suit of originality, independence and individuality, and untapped potential above all. Wands talk of all creative and artistic ventures, of male potency, travel, success, spontaneous house moves or relocations, health, self-confidence and self-esteem, independence, fame, and finding and following your unique path.

Wands advise focusing on your own needs and dreams, developing a creative talent, taking the lead at work or branching out with your own business or self-employment. They promise personal joy and fulfillment and any Wand's approach will be dynamic, spontaneous, intuitive, and inventive and will involve the unexpected.

Abundance and generosity are its virtues; fickleness and a tendency to give up at the first obstacle, impatience with human frailty, or boredom are its faults.

Swords, the Suit of Air; the World of the Mind and of Speculation

Swords are the suit of logic, focus, rational thought, courage, careers in organizations, examinations and tests, and change.

Swords talk of clear communication, speculation, all matters scientific and technological as well as conventional medicine, therapy and surgery, justice, learning, and the law. They may predominate in a reading at challenging times in your life and can refer to difficult people.

Swords advise using the mind (not the heart) and of speaking out. Any Sword's approach will be swift and courageous and single-minded and may involve disruptive but necessary change.

Learning and concentration are its virtues; unfounded fears in your mind that hold you back from action and being unduly harsh or critical are its negative side.

THE NUMBERS

Following are descriptions of the numbers one (or Ace) through ten.

The Aces, the New Beginning Cards

Aces, or ones, are the most dynamic cards of the Minor Arcana. One is the number of the innovator and initiator.

These cards always herald new opportunities, new people, or restored energies, good luck, and health coming into your life—in the area of your life indicated by the suit. It would be hard to find a negative meaning for an Ace. You can feel optimistic even if you are going through a bad patch when Aces appear, for your luck is turning for the better. More than one Ace in a general reading indicates a time of great opportunity.

What is more, the four Aces can be used independently of

the rest of the number cards in addition to the Major cards in any full reading to help you see how best to tackle the situations you face, according to the kind of Ace that appears. I call the four Aces used in this way the Mood cards because they are the key to the approach needed to make the message of the main reading work.

The Mood cards reflect the mood that you can channel to your best advantage.

The Ace of Pentacles, the Practical Solutions Card

This is the most stable of the Aces. The new opportunity will come within your existing life and cause gradual improvements. This card is good for all home projects, renovations, or planned moves, and for a safe, if slow, opportunity to put your finances on a more stable footing; any new business ventures or investments, practical or financial, are assured long-term success.

AS A MOOD CARD

There's hard work to be done and the only solution is a practical one, initiated by you. You are assured of success but there are no quick fixes or shortcuts. Start where you are, for your ideas have firm foundations and if you persevere will bring tangible results.

The Ace of Cups, the Following Your Heart Card

This is the card indicating new love and fertility. There may be a pregnancy or family addition, perhaps through marriage or remarriage; you may find new love or be entering a new happy phase in an existing relationship. This Ace may represent the regrowth of trust or of valuing yourself as you are, and perhaps a new friend or ally who will become important over the months. There may be a new peaceful phase in relationships with family and the resolution of a long-standing conflict. Occasionally, the Ace of Cups can signify unrequited love or one that must remain a secret.

AS A MOOD CARD

Listen to what lies behind people's words. Try to sort out what you feel about a person or situation. Do you feel comfortable with the people involved? Follow your gut feeling.

The Ace of Wands, the Inspiration Card

Anything is possible, usually what is least expected. Be optimistic.

Wish and your wish will come true; this card represents a chance to take an interest in a second career (or at least a lucrative hobby). Take up a creative activity, whether dance, music, art, or acting—or perhaps an interest you had abandoned years before. You may be offered a promotion, a relocation, or an unexpected holiday; a return to health, to enthusiasm, personal power, belief in your own abilities and—with such power you can't fail.

AS A MOOD CARD

Think outside the box and make an all-or-nothing leap to happiness, success, fame, or fulfillment.

The Ace of Swords, the Thinking and Then Acting Decisively Card

After a difficult time or setback, cut through inertia, doubts, and fears; start again and overcome any obstacles. This is a time for learning, training, or retraining; a satisfactory legal settlement, resolution of a neighborhood or work dispute, or winning overdue recognition of effort at work; a good outcome of medical or surgical procedures; and for risk-taking or games of chance.

AS A MOOD CARD

The situation calls for decisive action, but take a step back, think it through calmly and logically, then be prepared to confront negative people and less-than-honest situations head on, quietly and assertively, but without compromising your integrity. Truth will emerge.

USING YOUR FOUR ACE MOOD CARDS

Working at this stage with just the four Aces and the Major cards helps to fine-tune your intuitive tarot-reading powers.

Keep the four of Aces separate from the Major cards in a face-down pile to shuffle separately each time you do a reading of three or more cards.

As before, choose three, six, or nine cards and place them face-down in rows of three, left to right. Either turn the cards over one by one or altogether and build up the story, bottom to top.

Now mix the four Aces face-down and take one of them from the separate Ace pile. Turn this over and it will give you the best strategy to follow, or the overall energy of the reading.

4

THE
MINOR CARDS,
TWOS TO FIVES

I N THE PREVIOUS CHAPTER YOU USED THE ACES AS
Mood cards to give you strategies about to how to proceed with
the information given in a reading.

The number cards expand the meaning of any Major cards and
offer more detail about the influence of those around us on our lives
and the context and sometimes constraints within which we make
our decisions. What is more, all the number cards, not just the Aces,
offer strategies for any changes we would like to make in our lives
and highlight our hidden strengths and potential.

When selected as your card of the day that you pick in the
morning as a guide to the day ahead, number cards highlight specific
opportunities and challenges in the day ahead.

I: THE ACES, THE NEW BEGINNING CARDS

Read through the Aces in the previous chapter, focusing on their new-beginning aspect in order to remind yourself of their significance.

II: THE TWOS, THE BALANCE CARDS

Two represents integration of two people or two aspects of life and the best harmony between those two people or life paths. Two is the number of the negotiator and talks about balancing priorities and sometimes of the need to do more than one thing at once. It also relates to partnerships, both business and emotional.

The Two of Pentacles

The Two of Pentacles says it is possible to follow two paths at once, whether work and home, two different kinds of work, or a work and a hobby that may prove an extra source of income.

However, right now one aspect of your life, or one person, is taking priority over the others. This may be necessary, but trying to keep two people or situations balanced may mean you feel disharmonious or do neither thing properly.

The Two of Cups

Often associated with twin-soul love, two people or families coming together in reconciliation, harmony, or love, the Two of Cups can indicate a forthcoming engagement or commitment.

It can also be a quarrel that can be mended. For new love and a new relationship or for love as yet unrealized, the Two of Cups says the right person is not far away. It is also a good omen if partners, family, or close friends plan to work closely together.

The Two of Wands

Twos are unusually static cards for the dynamic Wands and suggest there are or will be two choices of life path, often a creative venture versus a secure path. It is necessary to choose and commit to one path, but wait and the right choice will become clear within a few weeks.

Sometimes the card can indicate that a current business partnership or work relationship may seem restrictive or a home situation safe but dull (occasionally an indication that a work flirtation is proving tempting). These basically stable situations need reviving rather than abandoning.

Overseas contacts or ventures may prove fruitful.

The Two of Swords

This is a card of being stuck between two options or people and feeling unable to decide between them or move. Fear within can be the obstacle.

Usually neither option is right and there is a third you have not considered. It could even be to go it alone or take the next step alone, cutting free of guilt within and emotional pressures around you.

The card can refer to financial problems and says they won't go away but they can be sorted, not easily, but by talking and asking for help.

A career in negotiations or seeking conciliation or mediation is favored.

III: THE THREES, THE INCREASED JOY OR OPPORTUNITY CARDS

Three represents building or rebuilding on previous situations or decisions. The direction of those new opportunities will appear if you look hard enough. It is a number traditionally associated with celebrations, marriage, pregnancy, and birth—or increasingly with acquiring a ready-made family.

Threes are excellent for all creative ventures.

The Three of Pentacles

This is an excellent card that talks about building up tangible resources (maybe after a past setback or delay). It promises that any venture you begin or are currently working on has firm foundations, though it is a step-by-step progress.

The card assures success with any property deal, do-it-yourself project, or renovation. It also augurs well for crafts and using the hands, whether as a job or interest. Finances will improve and hard work and attention to detail are essential for progress, and working with others is the best way ahead.

The Three of Pentacles can herald closer links with an older relative.

This is an excellent omen for mortgages, remortgages, loans, and rescheduling debts.

The Three of Cups

This is a card of fertility and abundance; it is a pregnancy or marriage card and one of family celebration. It can also indicate the return of someone to the family after an absence working away or because of an estrangement.

New friends come into your life or old ones return.

Working with children and counseling are favored.

The Three of Wands

Any plan or creative venture you have or plan to put into action in the near future will lead to an expansion of opportunities. People from further afield and overseas will offer new outlets for your talents and perhaps unexpected overseas travel. Striking out for independence and getting your own home, promotion, or a new and more fulfilling career are indicated.

If job hunting, expand your range of jobs and the physical area of your search. Any creative ventures you pursue will receive a favorable response.

The Three of Swords

This never predicts heartbreak, but it can warn you to beware of someone who seems too good to be true. You should use your head and logic if you are being emotionally pressured or manipulated. Learn to say no to unreasonable family, friends, and colleagues.

Watch that others do not drain your finances or persuade you to lend them money or that you enter a deal just to please someone.

This is a sign that it is good to go ahead with study or a training program or a new job.

Watch those who are nice to your face but may be gossiping or spreading rumors.

This is an excellent card for any surgical or medical intervention.

IV: THE FOURS, THE CAUTION CARDS

Fours explore the alternatives of taking a risk or of holding on to what you have now, and they often appear when you are wondering if there is more to life than security.

The Four of Pentacles

This four is the ultimate example of caution versus taking a chance. This represents living the happy enough life, but it may be that by taking a chance on investing in something that would bring you fulfillment rather than financial return, you will find joy now. With Pentacles, you know that risk will pay out in the long term, for this card often represents a short-term risk for a long-term gain that is not 100 percent certain.

Since this is also a family card, life quality could be improved by taking a chance on new pastures or spending money on leisure and pleasure.

It can indicate you are staying in a relationship or job for security but at the cost of your personal freedom and future love and self-growth and initiative.

The Four of Cups

The Four of Cups shows that you need to make decisions rather than let matters drift or let others make the decisions. This often concerns uncertainty about whether a lover is serious and whether to allow things to carry on or to ask for more and risk rejection. Better to test the waters, because then you can move forward to another lover if the current one is not right.

The Four of Cups may also suggest you are not fulfilled spiritually or personally in your life, living space, or work, and that it's time to decide what you want and go for it—what we regret most is what we never try and the current one may involve leaving familiar comforts.

The Four of Wands

The Four of Wands is idyllic and refers to the chance of moving to a place where you will be truly at home; the actual structure matters less than the joy of living your dream sooner rather than later (and does not even mean a conventional home; it could be a boat or a motor home).

This can also say you have or will soon achieve your personal ambitions and enjoy a moderate and satisfying success. However, as a four, it asks, "Do you want more, to aim higher maybe at the cost of comfort and ease or living where you are happy?"

The Four of Wands can appear midcareer or even as early retirement is approaching, and it says you can still find those rainbows, perhaps moving further afield or building your dream home.

This is also the card of working from home but that may involve temporarily disruptive changes.

The Four of Swords

This card involves fears that may hold us frozen from initiating change or speaking out against unfairness.

Usually there is a good reason for feeling unable to act: circumstance, people who depend on us, past betrayal, or reversal of fortune—and being a four, this may not be the time to act. This card reassures you that the fears in your head are far, far worse than the reality.

When you feel ready, use the power of the Swords to cut through fear and reach for what you want.

V: FIVE, THE WINNING THROUGH CARDS

Fives are communication, swift and successful action, and acquiring new knowledge or resources.

Fives say you have to deal positively with any situation as it is now, rather than the way you would like it to be. With effort and help, often from further afield or sources you haven't considered before, all will be resolved in ways you had not even envisaged but that are always right.

The Five of Pentacles

You are not getting the help and support you need from family, friends, or official channels, and it suggests that your worries are about money, the home, family matters, the education of a child, or the care of a sick or elderly family member.

The card says persist but try additional and alternative sources of assistance that can maybe help you to put on the pressure needed to get the appropriate resources.

The card can appear if you are overwhelmed with domestic or workplace responsibilities; insist others do their share.

The Five of Cups

A broken relationship could be mended, but do you want it, and if so, what changes do you need if it is to work? You may have hit a bad or dull patch in a long-term relationship; try to remove outside interference and get away together, maybe permanently. The card can also appear if you are involved in or tempted to begin an affair. Some people can be happy with two partners but sooner or later one of the relationships (or maybe both) will break under the strain.

The Five of Wands

This card indicates a time when you need to fight for what you want, whether a promotion at work or success in a competitive, artistic, or creative field—or for your identity if it is being eroded by the demands of others. A career in communication or the media would be successful. If work is overcompetitive or hostile, look elsewhere or go it alone.

The Five of Swords

This is a card of fighting and winning against difficult odds or obstacles.

Tackle obstacles or opposition calmly but make sure of your facts and your rights; it is a good card for getting justice. Watch out, however, for sneaky dealings or seeming friends who would stab you in the back.

If you are being emotionally manipulated, stop allowing others to press your buttons, and do not let people who play on their weakness sap your strength.

THE OPTIONS SPREAD

This remarkably simple layout is good when there are two or more options to decide between.

Card One: The Question

This represents the choice to be made or the issue that prompted the reading.

Select card one face-down from the face-down shuffled or mixed pack.

Do not turn over or read card one until you have dealt all the cards and assigned the option rows.

Cards Two through Seven: The Two Choices

First, decide which option will represent which choice. Deal these six cards face-down in pairs side by side, starting from just below card one. Deal vertically pair-by-pair toward you.

Turn over card one and see how it relates to the question. If this is not clear, deal a second card by the side of card one.

Turn over and read option one; then cards two, four, and six in that order, using the position meanings listed after the diagram as a guide.

Read the second row: option two; cards three, five, and seven.

Decide which seems the most viable choice.

If neither option feels right, add a third option row to the right of option two.

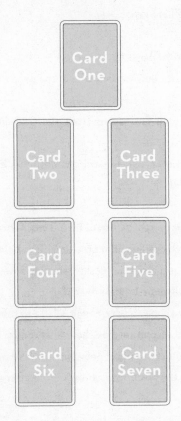

CARD ONE: The Question or issue about which of the choices are to be made.

CARD TWO: The Suggested Action you might take to carry out option one, the left-hand row.

CARD THREE: The Suggested Action for option two, the right-hand row.

CARD FOUR: The Unforeseen Consequences (either good or challenging) that result from carrying through option one.

CARD FIVE: The Unforeseen Consequences for option two.

CARD SIX: The Likely Outcome of following the path of option one.

CARD SEVEN: The Likely Outcome of option two.

A Real-Life Reading

Following is a description of an options reading using the method described in this chapter.

TOM'S STORY

Tom's girlfriend, Linda, had left him for the third time for another man. Now she wanted Tom back as her new relationship had gone disastrously wrong yet again. The two options he identified were to take Linda back or to go on alone.

Card one, the Question or Issue, was the Ace of Swords.

Card one asked Tom if he should logically start again after the frequent betrayals.

It is also a card of learning. Tom had been offered a major training course in his social-care profession, but it would involve him working two hundred miles away for six months. Linda, he knew, would never accept that.

Option one represented his decision to return to Linda (and turning the course down). Card two Suggested Action was the Lovers.

Taking Linda back would lead to a passionate reconciliation, but in the past, the honeymoon period was followed by Linda getting more discontented and eventually betraying him.

Card four, the Unforeseen Consequences of taking option one, was the Death card.

What would die? Tom's peace of mind, as he would always be watching for signs of future betrayal; and most of all, his career advancement would be in jeopardy. Yet Linda drew him in like a magnet; and when he was happy, it was idyllic.

Card six, the Likely Outcome of taking option one, was the Five of Cups.

Could she change? In his heart, Tom knew she would not. But he loved her and did not want to walk away.

Option two was going it alone and taking up a training course offered at work.

Card three, the Suggested Action for option two, was the Eight of Cups, in which the man in the card is shown walking away, toward the unknown.

In this case, Tom would be leaving behind an unsatisfactory emotional attachment (although he has invested a great deal in it) with sorrow because he still has strong feelings for Linda.

Card five, the Unforeseen Circumstances of taking option two, was the Ace of Cups, the new beginning in love. Though this could refer to Linda appreciating Tom if he is away for six months, this would more likely suggest he will meet someone new whom he could grow to love.

Card seven, the Likely Outcome of taking option two, was the Emperor. This power card refers to Tom (whose power has been taken by Linda) focusing on his career so he can go a long way.

Tom asked Linda if she would come and live with him in town but she refused and insisted he give it up if he loved her. Tom said no, passed the training course with flying colors, was offered an excellent job, and now is engaged to a social worker he met in the course.

5

THE MINOR CARDS, SIX TO TEN

THE SIXES TO TENS ARE THE CARDS THAT SHOW we move through harmony and change to ultimate victory and endings, leading to beginnings.

VI: THE SIXES, THE HARMONY AND BALANCE CARDS

Sixes explore different ways of maintaining or achieving balance in your life within yourself. They promise that everything in your life will turn out better than expected.

But sixes can appear when you are regretting the past and dreaming about the future rather than focusing on fixing the present. You may also be waiting for perfect love and happiness rather than enjoying a real love or an existing relationship, even with the odd flaw.

The Six of Pentacles

Right now you may be giving out more than you are getting back, whether in financial terms, practical help, or appreciation. This is often family-related, but it can refer to a work situation in which you are left with all the responsibility and no credit.

It can also refer to personal cash-flow problems caused by your subsidizing family members or friends well able to sort out their own finances or by propping up a business that is better let go.

Speculation and jobs in finance, banking, or hands-on care, especially with older people are favored.

The Six of Cups

This is a card that promises happy, lasting love and especially having a family and finding a settled home; if you are older, it says you are with the right person but may not have found your dream home or lifestyle.

It can also indicate an addition to the family, whether through birth or an extra member coming with a new partner or new step-in-laws and this will be harmonious.

Finally, it can herald a return of a face from the past, or unexpected contact with childhood friends—even a former love.

The Six of Wands

This card sees you riding home in victory, maybe in six weeks or maybe in six months—the time frame depends on the question and the cards surrounding it. Persevere and you will succeed in that creative venture, career leap, travel dream, or bid for freedom; this is the card of finding harmony through fulfilling your unique vision and standing out from the crowd.

The Six of Swords

Calmer, more prosperous and happier times are ahead after a period of unrest, uncertainty, or sometimes great effort, so long as you leave behind any bitterness or regrets.

The card can also indicate beneficial travel, usually within six months, whether a holiday, relocation, or house move that will bring you happiness. Alternatively, a disruptive neighbor or a spiteful colleague will soon move unexpectedly out of your life.

VII: THE SEVENS, THE CONTEMPLATION CARDS

Seven is the number of wisdom, spirituality, and mystery. Rather than rushing or being hurried into a decision or change, wait until you are ready, as you may discover you are happy with your life as it is.

Trust your intuition and dreams. This card represents a period when your psychic development and healing powers will evolve naturally.

Beware of illusion, whether the easy path or being deceived by others against your better judgment.

The Seven of Pentacles

This is a long-term security card indicating stability through money or property that will continue to grow over seven years and beyond. This card indicates a good time to buy a home or invest in land, property, or safe investments as opposed to speculative investments.

The fruits of shorter-term effort or investment of time and resources will begin to show results even within six or seven months, and money or family worries will gradually improve over the same time scale.

The Seven of Cups

This represents opportunities in a career or venture that really matters to you or in opportunity in your relationships; these will involve making choices that should be made with the heart rather than the head.

You may be questioning a love commitment that is slow coming or seems unreliable or an issue of trust; ask questions rather than worrying. It may be that you discover the fears were within your own mind because you doubt yourself. Someone close will benefit from alternative and natural healing methods. Don't let others influence those choices.

The Seven of Wands

Here the choice is clear: stake your claim, find your base, or uproot and start again, somewhere new. Doing nothing is not an option.

This is also a success card, though you may first have to defend your position, argue your case, or fight off opposition. It can reveal a sudden chance at leadership, so stay alert to opportunity and do not underestimate your abilities.

The Seven of Swords

This card warns against double-dealing by others and people going behind your back.

If finances, custody issues, or property are under dispute, especially in a divorce settlement, make sure that you are well represented and watch your opponent for lies or signs that assests are being concealed. If business dealings have gone wrong, you will in the future recoup, if not reclaim, losses. When you are affected by gossip or troublesome neighbors, or have doubts about a lover who has betrayed you before, do not be fobbed off with excuses or someone putting the blame on you.

Don't fall for a too-good-to-be-true offer or a chance to make fast money.

VIII: THE EIGHTS, THE OPPORTUNITY AND LEARNING CARDS

Eights are the active, entrepreneurial cards of maximizing opportunities and overcoming obstacles and restrictions. They also talk of turning your back on what no longer works or on past matters that still haunt you, of learning new things, and of discovering new faces and places.

Speculation and risk taking will lead to a rapid increase of assets.

The Eight of Pentacles

Called the Apprentice or the self-employed card, this card promises that you can make your fortune by your own efforts. This is the right time to learn a new skill or develop an interest into a successful business.

Within an existing satisfactory career, the card can herald an opportunity to move into another field within the same firm or organization or to take extra responsibility. It also bodes well for any do-it-yourself project or house renovations.

If you have been practicing a skill or talent for a while, now is the time to test it publicly—and make money from it.

The Eight of Cups

This is a "walking away from what did not work" card, whether a destructive relationship, bad habit, job that has made you unhappy, or home you feel is not right for you. Yet this card is also about walking toward something that will make you happy and fulfilled, which may involve travel or even relocation.

There may also be reconciliation after a betrayal or temporary separation, but under new and more stable circumstances that must be determined by you.

It can also indicate a period working away from home that will prove advantageous; it's a good omen for a long-distance relationship.

The Eight of Wands

This is the ultimate "up and flying" card, indicating usually unexpected and fulfilling travel opportunities, a holiday, or especially long-distance or long-term ventures.

An Eight of Wands can indicate a fortunate career change involving a house move, visiting friends or relations abroad, or a new holiday home, boat, or vehicle.

This card alludes to a chance for developing exciting, unusual interests, meeting new and stimulating people, successful networking—especially in cyber space—and in business entrepreneurial ventures, reaching a far wider market. It may also portend recognition in the performing arts—"getting that big break."

The Eight of Swords

This is a card of restrictions—whether imposed by others, your own fears, or negative voices from the past—to be overcome only with effort and determination.

A setback can be used for new opportunity through the freedom of escaping from limitations and prohibitions that may have become a habit.

What you most fear—whether a job loss, someone leaving you, or losing money—will not happen but ask yourself if you actually want to be in the situation you are in. This card is good for overcoming addictions, fears, and phobias.

IX: THE NINES, THE SELF-FULFILLMENT CARDS

These are the cards of the self, self-confidence, independence, and, above all, self-reliance. They also represent striving for and attaining what you most want and completing a project successfully, especially a creative or independent one that will bring you freedom; do not accept second best in love, career, and life, for you can attain those dreams with one more supreme effort.

The Nine of Pentacles

This is sometimes called the card of fulfillment of wishes and of attaining security in money. You can succeed through your own efforts and don't need favors or to rely on the goodwill of others. Whether a family matter, financial issue, or a business venture, financial independence is assured if you do things your way.

Since nine is also a number of perfection, the card can refer to the achievement of a long-standing ambition. It is also another successful self-employment card.

You may have to help a friend or family member to become self-reliant (even if this involves tough love) do not bail out family members or friends financially who do not help themselves. Above all, you may want to build up your own private pot of money.

The Nine of Cups

The Nine of Cups is the ultimate independence from emotional pressures, helping you discover your personal power and desires within a relationship if you have relied on or needed the approval of others.

Right now you may need to focus on work or personal fulfillment and a relationship may temporarily have to take back seat; this can occur when a woman with children goes back to work and feels guilty about neglecting her family.

It can also occur if someone needs a period alone, perhaps after a breakup. Rather than rushing into a rebound affair, you may find you enjoy independence and want this even within a future relationship.

The Nine of Wands

This is often called the "almost there" card. It represents imminent triumph after a career struggle or a creative or artistic success, perhaps after a period of rejection or setbacks.

If you are still struggling and wonder if it is worthwhile, this is the card that tells you to be courageous. Victory is assured, though you may need to spread your net further and make an all-out push. It can also mean a return to health after an illness, accident, or exhaustion.

The Nine of Swords

The Nine of Swords refers to fears that have a firm foundation, opposition, and emotional as well as financial pressures. However, it promises that all will be well if you tackle problems and bullies head on, ignore gossip and rumor-mongering, logically consider the best option even if it is not ideal, and go for it. This is an anti-debt card that tells you to look for independent advice, because, however overwhelming, financial and housing problems can be resolved if you do not ignore bills and official documents.

Beware emotional vampires who suck your energies with their problems; if you are working in a hostile atmosphere, try to move on—and in the meantime do not get sucked into the toxic atmosphere.

X: THE TENS, THE COMPLETION OR CLOSURE CARDS

Tens are cards that promise successful completion of any matters or ambitions and long-term happiness and security in your life. This may involve closing doors in order to move into the next cycle and clear what is no longer needed, shedding old burdens, activities, and even people who hold you back or resent your success, in order to maximize your hard-won benefits.

The Ten of Pentacles

The Ten of Pentacles is the card of long term-happiness, security, and family joy. Whatever money or family worries you have right now, everything will turn out well; security and happiness will last into old age. It is a welcome card if you are hoping to start a family or settle down or if you plan to work with animals or have pets.

For people about to retire, it can herald a move abroad, or if you are younger, a new business venture as a couple, often home based;

practical, craft-based ventures or hospitality are favored.

Don't be tempted to stray if your present relationship is going through a bad patch; stick with loyal friends rather than exciting but fickle new ones.

The Ten of Cups

The Ten of Cups is the ultimate love card and speaks to lasting love and fidelity, rather than the material, secure aspects of a relationship. With the previous card present in a reading, the Ten of Cups completes future happiness in every way.

Follow your heart, even if that means giving up security or someone who promises you everything—except love—or who does not stir your passion.

The Ten of Cups can herald a sudden rekindling of passion after a period in which there has been little connection or that a relationship has reached a point when the next step must be a permanent commitment or heralds moving in together if that relationship is to flourish. The card is a good indication for the resolution of a secret love or love when one or both parties are not free.

It can also promise happiness through children and grandchildren and working with children in a care or therapeutic situation.

The Ten of Wands

The card says that the end result of your creative or career endeavor, your travel plans, or personal dreams are within sight. Drop those aspects of your life that have become redundant, unfulfilling, or hold you back from realizing these hard-won dreams.

It also promises sudden and unexpected support or financial help if you need backing in order to put a dream into practice.

The card is an assurance that good health will be restored to you or a loved one.

The Ten of Swords

This is a symbol of a necessary ending, leading to a new beginning when a relationship or career path is going nowhere. You need to be strong and not allow yourself to be emotionally manipulated or be bullied or to stay in a no-hope situation out of misplaced loyalty or guilt. There really is light at the end of the tunnel.

If anyone you know will soon have an operation or any surgical or medical treatment, this card is an excellent omen.

THE CROSSROADS SPREAD

Try the Crossroads Spread if you have come to a change point in life, a "what next?" if the way ahead seems uncertain or you feel you have lost direction.

Usually, at the end of the reading you return to card one (the original question) and reassess if you want any change in light of cards two through five, and if so when and how.

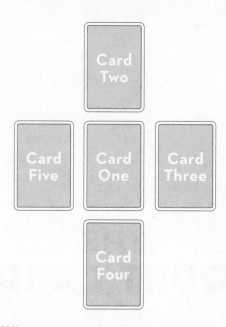

CARD ONE: Where you are now?

CARD TWO: What will be gained? The advantages of change.

CARD THREE: What will be lost? The disadvantages of change.

CARD FOUR: Who or what will help you to make a desired change?

CARD FIVE: Who or what will hinder you if you make a desired change?

CARD ONE: Reassessment: Is the change worthwhile and if so when?

CARD SIX: Optional and pulled from the whole pack if card one needs clarification.

Turn over and read each card one after the other. You will find that you view card one differently at the end of the reading. If not, focus on the question again and pick your sixth card to cover the first one.

6

THE
COURT CARDS

THE FINAL SIXTEEN CARDS ARE CALLED THE Court cards, four for each suit, a Page or Princess, a Knight or Prince, Queen, and King. They represent people in our world, family members, lovers, children, friends, foes, employers, managers, or influential colleagues. The names of the cards may differ slightly in various packs but are always easily identifiable. Court cards can also signify qualities, strengths, and challenges in your life or those of loved ones.

READING THE COURT CARDS

After you have read the card meanings, identify each of the sixteen characters in your life, past or present. Also ask yourself which card you are most like right now and who you would like to become.

The Pages/Princesses

Pages refer to a girl or a sensitive boy, a younger teenager of either sex, or a young adult woman who is not in a committed relationship or in a settled home of her own—or acts like a spoiled princess.

The card can also represent an undeveloped aspect of the questioner's personality or talent that is emerging or the first tentative steps toward a new life phase or activity.

The challenging aspect of Pages is when they represent someone of any age who is deliberately acting helpless or is being very childish and stubborn (and it's more common than you'd think to get fifty-year-old Pages!).

THE PAGE/PRINCESS OF PENTACLES

If a person in your life, the Page of Pentacles indicates someone young or young for his or her age, who is nevertheless trustworthy, patient, even-tempered, calm, and hard-working, and who is very reliable with money.

As a characteristic, this Page indicates learning a craft or skill or beginning a long course of study that will progress step by step. It can also herald a new financial beginning after a setback.

The only challenging aspect is an unwillingness to try new things or go to new places.

THE PAGE/PRINCESS OF CUPS

If a person in your life, the Page of Cups is very sensitive, kind, imaginative, trustworthy, idealistic, and psychic and it heralds a first or slowly blossoming love match.

As a characteristic, the Page of Cups heralds the slow regrowth of trust in life and love after betrayal and also learning something new for which you have a passion or developing spirituality and healing skills.

The challenging aspect is setting people on pedestals and being bitterly disillusioned when they prove to be human. These Pages are also easily conned.

THE PAGE/PRINCESS OF WANDS

If a person in your life, the Page of Wands of any age is constantly changing mood, moving location, seeking new activities and friends, and then moving on to the next wonder of life, seemingly on a whim.

As a characteristic, the Page of Wands signifies the emergence of a new creative dream and being unwilling to commit to a particular path but dashing from one to an ever-more exciting opportunity.

The challenging aspect is distractibility and impatience of waiting for ideas to develop.

THE PAGE/PRINCESS OF SWORDS

If a person in your life, the Page of Swords is too clever for his or her own good, challenging authority for the sake of it, and hurting feelings through thoughtlessness.

As a characteristic, the Page of Swords represents rejecting help, advice, and affection because of a past hurt and fighting for causes not worth championing.

The challenging aspect is overdefensiveness and seeing slights when there are none intended.

The Knights or Princes

Knights/Princes are older teenage boys. They can also represent young men who are still uncommitted or men of any age who retain their desire for freedom—even if committed.

The card as a characteristic signifies enthusiasm and impetus for a venture or a life change that will bring freedom and personal fulfillment. In love, Knights represent a slow-growing relationship, at any age or stage.

The challenging aspect is selfishness, whatever the age of the Knight (men especially in midlife crisis can revert to Knights).

THE KNIGHT/PRINCE OF PENTACLES

If a person in your life, the Knight of Pentacles is conservative and will not stray too far from home or familiar pursuits. This Knight perseveres in order to develop a solid career and will save carefully to get on the property ladder; also a faithful but inarticulate lover.

As a characteristic, the Knight of Pentacles represents a sound plan for a money-spinning venture and perseverance with slow-moving affairs or difficult people.

The challenging aspect is an unwillingness to express differing opinions or to take risks on money or love.

THE KNIGHT/PRINCE OF CUPS

As a person in your life, this is your knight in shining armor: romantic, idealistic, and dreamy; an excellent potential twin soul love that will grow over the years.

As a characteristic, the Knight of Cups heralds true love and coming romance, or if you are contemplating a secret love affair; also learning a spiritual or people-based art that can develop into a career.

The challenge is the romantic who never grows up and leaves a trail of broken hearts and shattered dreams, his own as well as others'.

THE KNIGHT/PRINCE OF WANDS

As a person in your life, the charismatic but somewhat unreliable Knight of Wands constantly changes course for new and ever-more-exciting and perilous quests.

A great speculator and communicator who can talk himself out of tight corners, as well as an entrepreneur, this Knight achieves success early but sometimes loses it just as fast—and then makes it again.

As a characteristic, the Knight of Wands represents the desire to travel and to fulfill dreams at any age and cost, and if necessary, shed commitments that are burdensome.

This Knight's challenging aspect is his unwillingness to stick at anything routine, and he may dump a loyal friend or love for someone more exciting.

THE KNIGHT/PRINCE OF SWORDS

As a person in your life, the Knight of Swords is totally single-minded in his goals, whether an enterprise or person; others have to get out of the way or get hurt.

Remarkably clever, especially in technology, medicine, or science, but sarcastic, these Knights are easily offended and slow to forgive. However, they can be a tremendous force for good if wisely directed.

As a characteristic, the Knight of Swords helps fight fearlessly against injustice, but will never compromise or accept frailty or imperfection in self or others.

His challenging aspect is that he hurts the innocent as well as himself.

The Queens

Queens represent older women, whether in age or maturity. They aren't necessarily mothers but are settled in their own home base or caring for others, either professionally or personally.

They can also be a female authority figure and can refer to caring men who occupy a professional or personal nurturing role toward others.

As a characteristic, the card signifies fertile (not just in the sense of babies) period; a chance to use your creative skills to help, advise, or protect others, or carve out a new second career or take over a ready-made family.

The challenging aspect of the Queens is possessiveness, or defining yourself only in terms of others' happiness.

THE QUEEN OF PENTACLES

As a person, she is Queen of Hearth and Home and also a successful businesswoman, often balancing both. She may be a mother, grand-mother, or head of a company or department involved in the care of others or she may be a nurturing manager.

She cares for others in a practical way, rather than with sympathy, and sticks to responsibilities and commitments no matter how tired or busy she is. As a characteristic, the Queen of Pentacles appears at a settled period in your life or a period when you are turning an interest into a full-scale venture.

Her challenging side is that she does too much for others and becomes a martyr, finding it hard to delegate.

THE QUEEN OF CUPS

As a person in your life, this is the ultimate Queen of Hearts, the mistress of love and of fertility who is also oversensitive to disharmony in her work or family life.

She is a fertility symbol, is incredibly psychic and healing, and in matters of love represents a woman who is deeply loved or who will find lasting love soon. As a characteristic, the Queen of Cups says you are ready to make a permanent commitment or that the person you are with is right; she also indicates a successful career/business in the spiritual, counseling, or therapeutic arts.

Her challenge is in fearing to let go of those she loves or of loving too much. She also sees the world through rose-colored spectacles.

THE QUEEN OF WANDS

As a person in your life, this fiery, creative Queen is inspiring, full of ideas, and open to adventure and travel. Always her own woman, though she can be an inspiring mother and loyal partner, she is naturally very creative, needing a stimulating career, and she likes to be her own boss.

As a characteristic, this Queen heralds a strong desire for independence and the chance to earn a good living through creativity or communication, but for her, fulfillment is more important than money.

Her challenging traits are lacking patience with others' weaknesses and knowing she is always right.

As a person, this Queen is an icon of female power, determined to win in spite of any obstacles and, above all, to learn new things. She is emotionally strong, is clever, and has overcome great odds and can be incredibly loyal, although she may seem unsympathetic or overcritical and bitter.

However, she can appear as a difficult manipulative ex-partner or mother who causes problems.

As a characteristic, the Queen of Swords represents a sudden surge in power to overcome abuse or injustice and she bodes well if you are taking up study, training, or retraining later in life.

Her challenging aspect is that life has soured her and she resents the happiness of others and uses emotional blackmail to manipulate others through guilt.

The Kings

Kings represent mature or older men, fathers, grandfathers, mentors, or authority figures, either an actual person (such as a bank manager or financial official) or an institution (such as a legal one). In a love relationship, they are or will be a permanent partner.

As a characteristic, Kings symbolize power, success, and the determination to achieve a particular goal that may be difficult but will bring great rewards and increased prosperity. They can also apply to women who are ambitious and seeking to make it to the top.

The Kings' challenging aspects are inflexibility, dogmatism, and stubbornness, being judgmental and, at worst, a bully.

THE KING OF PENTACLES

This reliable and wise King offers stability and practical as well as material security and is the ideal husband, father, grandfather, understanding bank manager, honest broker, and fair-minded employer.

As a person in your life, the King of Pentacles offers reliability and is—or will one day be—financially successful in his career. He may well have a steady business.

As a characteristic, this card can emerge when you are setting up a longer-term business or property venture or conducting renovations or working your way to senior levels in an official organization and this card is an assurance of success.

The challenging aspect of this king is obsession with making money and railroading others into following his blueprint for life. The King of Pentacles can also be set in his ways and resistant to travel.

THE KING OF CUPS

As a person, the King of Hearts represents lasting love and fidelity through good and hard times.

He is good with children, animals, and older people and may be overgenerous with time, resources, or money—not always to worthy causes.

As a characteristic, this may represent a choice between an old and established love and a new love, when the heart will win. It may alternatively indicate that now is the time for a major commitment in a relationship—and this card may say it will be forever.

The challenging aspects of this King is dreaming of the ideal, as well as missing or abandoning existing but slightly imperfect happiness. A crisis in confidence midlife can make him susceptible to flattery.

THE KING OF WANDS

As a person, the Sun King is a visionary, a successful creator, a salesperson and entrepreneur, a natural leader, and an inventor. He is a lifetime traveler and, as a husband and father, will bring fun, variety, and an unconventional lifestyle.

As a characteristic, the King of Wands says to go all out for fame, fulfillment, and fortune, spreading the net as far as possible, especially in cyber space, to reach new markets and audiences.

The challenging side of this King is a lack of awareness of the needs and feelings of others (he is a one-man show), fickleness, a tendency to flirt, and arrogance toward those he considers boring or stupid.

THE KING OF SWORDS

As a person, the King of Swords is a champion of truth, justice, and impartiality and he cannot be swayed by fear or favor. However, he finds expressing emotions hard and is usually a taciturn father, grandfather, or husband, although he would lay down his life for his family.

As an authority figure, whether connected with the law, the field of taxation, the medical profession, or a government body, the King of Swords is impatient of inefficiency but will offer support against corruption no matter how elevated the status of the wrongdoer.

As a characteristic, the King of Swords represents the power to overcome bullying and injustice through legal or official means and promises success in examinations or assessments. Double-checking facts and figures brings desired results.

His challenging aspects include overriding others' opinions, sarcasm, and occasionally cruelty or abusive behavior.

THE COURT CARD PERSONALITIES SPREAD

Reading the Court Cards with this spread can help give insight into individual personalities and solve personal problems. Follow the steps to use the Court Card Personalities for a reading.

Shuffle the sixteen Court cards and place them face-down in a circle, dealt clockwise.

Hold your hands over the cards one by one and select the four cards that feel right and place them in a face-down pile and shuffle.

Dealing from the top, place a card face-down nearest to you. Read this and then place the second card directly above the first, reading this before selecting the third until you have read the four cards in a vertical pathway.

CARD FOUR: Who you become.

CARD THREE: Who will oppose you.

CARD TWO: Who will help you.

CARD ONE: Who you are now.

A Real-Life Reading

Read for an account of how reading the Court Card personalities helped navigate an interpersonal quandary.

ADAM'S STORY

Adam is working his way up the corporate ladder but has discovered that an older female senior manager has feelings for him. She has been giving him access to secret information that will fast-track his career, but she has made it clear she wants a sexual relationship in return. Adam knows this is not right, but he is desperate to further his career quickly because his father has been ill and Adam has been helping the family financially. The manager has made it clear that if he does not comply, she will report Adam for breaking into confidential files. Following are the results of Adam's reading using the Court Card personalities.

CARD ONE: Who are you now: Page of Cups: Not even a Prince but a rather foolish young page, who for the best motives has compromised himself and now feels trapped.

CARD TWO: Who will help you: The King of Pentacles: This represents the senior director of the company, who greatly values some special work Adam had done in his own time and has been asking Adam if he would go away for six months on a special course on his present salary but with all expenses paid; this would bring a better job in a completely different wing of the company, which would take him right away from the toxic female and would enable him to send money home.

CARD THREE: Who will oppose you: The Queen of Swords: The senior female manager is spiteful and does not reflect love, only control. Adam has heard that other young male employees have been threatened by her; and so with unusual bravery, Adam said that he would be prepared to track down these other employees, who had all left under a cloud.

CARD FOUR: What you will become: King of Wands: Not straight away of course, but this showed that Adam has the potential to succeed in the new direction he is being offered, given perseverance.

To clarify a position, you can pull extra cards to answer any "what-ifs." Adam chose a card for what he would become if he went along with the Queen of Swords. The answer was a Page of Swords, without power, disappointed, and without love.

Adam accepted the training and when the manager threatened him, he told her he had evidence of other young men who had suffered sexual harassment at her hands and he intended to make a complaint based on their evidence. To his amazement, she backed down and told him she never wanted to see him again.

7

TAROT SPREADS FOR EVERY OCCASION

THERE ARE MANY SPREADS OR LAYOUTS YOU can use in tarot reading. Although the ones I suggest work well for me and a number of other readers, it is important to make them right for you. Therefore, adapt the names of any card positions that seem irrelevant or unhelpful and add or remove card positions that do not instinctively fit.

A HORSESHOE SPREAD

This five-card layout can be used with the Major Arcana or the whole pack. It is good for a matter or situation in which you want to see the longer-term outcome of actions that are suggested within the spread.

Deal five cards in a horseshoe formation face-down from the shuffled pack, card one to card five.

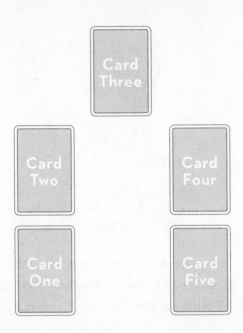

The Cards

CARD ONE: The Issue: Your present position and either the choice, dilemma, or predominant question about a central aspect of your life.

CARD TWO: Present Influences: These are circumstances and people who have contributed to your present position and who would be affected by any decision or change you make.

CARD THREE: Unexpected Influences: These may be hidden factors, past successes, old fears, or the messages we carry in our head from parents, past lovers, etc. They also include those influences we can sense just over the horizon that will come into play according to whether we decide to change or preserve the status quo.

CARD FOUR: Suggested action: This offers an action, move, or tactic that will further the situation under question.

CARD FIVE: Possible outcome: This suggests the potential consequences of our intervention or actions.

There is the option to add a sixth card above and between cards one and five to reveal what would happen if we did not act.

Either formulate a specific question or, if matters are unclear, let your mind go blank and allow the first card dealt to provide the real question.

Shuffle the deck and deal the five cards face-down.

Read the cards from the bottom left one at a time before turning over the next: card one, then upward and down the other side of the horseshoe to the bottom right (card five).

THE CALENDAR SPREAD: TWELVE MONTHS OF THE YEAR

Although you use a lot of cards in this spread, the method and interpretation are remarkably simple. You can start at any time of the year, but it is especially good to begin in a birthday month or as a special New Year's reading. Personal change points are also potent: anniversaries, engagements, a wedding, or the birth of a child—or if you are newly divorced, to give you hope for the year ahead.

As well as twelve months, if you have a crucial period you can also pick cards for the seven days ahead or the twenty-eight, twenty-nine, thirty, or thirty-one days of the month you are asking about.

For a twelve-month prediction or the month ahead spread, it can be helpful to mix two tarot packs together because, if a card recurs, you will know that it has particular significance in your life.

First, decide on the period you are predicting to determine the number of cards you will need to select. From a face-down shuffled or mixed pack (or two packs mixed together), select the required number of cards and set the cards clockwise face-down in a circle.

Turn each card over in a clockwise direction and read it before turning over the next. As you choose each card, if reading for yourself hold it and allow images, ideas, words, or impressions, to come naturally. Write or record your impressions, and each card will guide you as to the opportunities or particular challenges you may face during the individual period.

If reading for others, ask the questioner to hold the chosen card before holding it yourself; then read each card aloud and, again, as it is an extensive reading, you may wish to record the results for the person to take home.

On the whole, Major Arcana cards indicate major events or instances in which outside circumstances play a big part. Minor cards refer to more ordinary but, nevertheless, significant happenings occurring in the period you are measuring. Court cards indicate dominant personalities—or maybe when a new love or pregnancy will come, if that is what you are seeking.

When you have finished your calendar spread, choose a final card to sum up the seven days, the month, or the twelve months ahead and put this in the center of the circle.

Start card one at the time frame where you begin the reading.

THE GYPSY SPREAD

Sometimes used with playing cards, this nine-card spread is one of the old Romany layouts that involve the whole pack. This is an especially good formula for love, relationships, major moves, or career issues. It can also be easily adapted for questions of justice or financial matters. Although slightly more complex, and therefore a transition to the complex spreads in the final chapter, it builds on what you have already learned and is very straightforward.

The Method

Shuffle or mix the cards, choose three from the face-down pack, and lay out these three cards face-down, left to right, as row one.

Turn the cards over from left to right. Before reading, lay out above the first row a second row and then a third row above the second, each of three cards, always left to right. Turn over the second row before selecting the third. Read from bottom left to top right.

ROW 1: THE CARDS OF YOUR RELATIONSHIP OR CAREER

These first three cards concern your current or projected relationship, career, or home location as it is now, as well as any questions or doubts you may have.

CARD ONE: Past events moving away.

CARD TWO: Present sticking points or doubts.

CARD THREE: What you most want from the relationship/career/move.

ROW 2: THE CARDS OF OUTSIDE INFLUENCES

These show the influences of others on a relationship or potential relationship, whether opposition, pressures to marry, relatives, ex-partners and stepchildren, people who may further or block your career, or people who are involved in location choices.

CARD FOUR: Positive aspects and people.

CARD FIVE: Hidden opposition.

CARD SIX: What must be overcome.

ROW 3: THE CARDS OF ACTION AND OUTCOME

The final three cards offer the way forward and will contain an inbuilt solution, but if in doubt, add a tenth and eleventh card above row three for clarifying the relative losses and gains.

CARD SEVEN: Suggested action.

CARD EIGHT: Short-term outcome.

CARD NINE: Long-term outcome.

8

FINDING YOUR OWN STYLE OF TAROT READING

THERE ARE MANY MISCONCEPTIONS ABOUT THE tarot. Earlier we dispelled the myth that it is unlucky to buy your own tarot pack. However, while it is lovely to be given a pack as a present, it is far better to go into a bookstore, to visit a New Age store, or go online and find the pack that is right for you. If in doubt, start with one of the Waite-inspired packs, such as the Rider Waite, Universal Waite, or Golden Waite, which are named after their creator, A. E. Waite, and have inspired many other decks. Later, you can choose one depicting Celtic figures, medieval lords and ladies, or something more modern if you prefer. There are a huge number of examples online of different tarot packs with descriptions and images.

Take as long as you want learning individual cards or experimenting with the new layouts I have described so far in this book. If any spreads feel difficult or not right, leave them and try them later, accepting that some methods will feel better for you than others will.

REVERSALS

Yet another tarot myth is that cards that are drawn from the pack upside down represent a bad aspect of the card or a weakening of the meaning. Every card has both positive and challenging aspects within it. The reason a card is reversed is because it was put back that way in the pack during the previous session. The other cards in the reading will determine whether an individual card's challenging or positive aspect is most in evidence.

GIVING DEPTH TO READINGS

It is no more difficult to mix two identical packs and read with them than to use one. If you prefer, keep the two card packs separate and alternately take from both so you always have the required number of cards in total.

The advantage of a double pack is that if the same card appears twice in different positions, you know it is of particular significance. You can also use two different kinds of tarot cards, as then the alternative image can give you an extra perspective on a repeated card. For example, in the Druidcraft Tarot, the conventional Wheel of Fortune is shown as a woman drawing her own wheel in the sand, a very different meaning from the turning Wheel of Fate.

SUBSTITUTIONS

If any card that is dealt appears unhelpful to the questioner, or if a card refers to a past issue best forgotten or that needs to be removed from his or her life, ask the questioner to pick a substitute card from the face-down pack.

Set this on top of the card you wish to replace. This may be a transition card, so if the card you substitute still feels like only part of the story, substitute yet another card until you and the questioner feel you have the right answer, placing each new card on top of the one you are replacing. This can especially occur in cards in the Action position or an Outcome card position.

READING FOR YOURSELF

You can just as easily and accurately read the Tarot for yourself as for others, in spite of superstitions that claim this is unlucky. The cards you choose will guide you in your personal readings, and card readings are an excellent way of giving you information that others may be hiding. You may find it best when reading for yourself to record the session and just talk freely about what you see, hear, or feel for each card.

This stops your logical mind tidying up and analyzing the meaning of the reading. Then play back the recording with the layout in front of you.

READING FOR OTHERS

When you read for others, ask the person what he or she wants to know. Yet another misconception is that the tarot reader should guess what the other person wants to know. While the cards will indicate areas of concern, guessing is time consuming, rather like going to a doctor and saying, "Hey, Doc, guess what is wrong with me."

Of course, a doctor would diagnose the problem by elimination, but a tarot reading is best used to look for hidden factors and solutions.

Start from an initial focus or area of concern, such as love life or career, to help you and the questioner tune in to each other. Ask the person whose cards you are reading to shuffle, mix, or select the cards face-down and to give the correct number of cards to you face-down.

As you turn each card, ask the questioner what he or she feels about the card and what is seen in each picture. Then explain what you are feeling, but ensure that you keep a dialogue going as this not only keeps the psychic energies flowing between you but also it will encourage the person for whom you are reading to make his or her own decisions.

That is the purpose of a reading: that others can see what they may have instinctively felt but doubted to be the correct path, which is now confirmed in the cards.

IF A READING IS NOT WORKING

If you are using a three-, six-, or nine-card reading without positions, add more cards one at a time till it makes sense (usually three additional cards at the most will clarify even the most complex issue).

For a reading in which there are set positions, put all the cards chosen together once more in a face-down pile, shuffle or mix them, and then deal them face-down in rows of three, left to right, bottom to top, till you run out of cards.

Then take from the main pack however many cards are needed to complete the top row.

Turn them all over in order of dealing and read bottom to top, left to right, as though telling a story. This never fails.

CARD OF THE DAY

Earlier in the book, I talked about picking a card of the day every day and recording it in your tarot journal so you can see any repetitions that would indicate a matter or person in your life who demands action.

If a particular card appears on the same day every week or month, try to work out what happens on that day. If necessary, add two cards to the repeated card and do a three-card reading.

DOING READINGS WITH CARDS OF THE DAY

If you have had a particularly significant week and want to understand underlying currents that are not clear with loved ones, friends, or colleagues—especially if you are coming up to a decision or change—take the seven cards that you picked during the previous week as your cards of the day.

If the same card recurs during the week, read that card for the day it first appeared and then leave a gap so you can place it and read it again later in the reading for the day it recurred (moving the same card up the layout as many days as it recurs). Make two left-to-right rows of three, plus one at the top, leaving a gap for any recurring card. Day one will be bottom left and day seven at the top. Turn over each card in turn, read it, and carry on until you have read all seven days. If a card is repeated on a number of days, you know it is of significance.

9

MORE COMPLEX SPREADS TO DEVELOP YOUR TAROT SKILLS

SOME TAROT READERS BELIEVE THE MORE COMPLEX a layout, the better the tarot reading. This is not so. However, the reason for using a layout with a lot of cards and/or a larger number of card positions is that it gives additional information if you are doing a life review for yourself or someone else or are at a major life change or face a life-or-death decision. The two layouts or spreads that follow can be broken down into simple stages so that you can learn them step by step.

Only use these complex spreads for yourself once a month at the most. If you read for the same person regularly, only do these longer layouts monthly or at major change points in his or her life. Most useful is to check up every three months about how things are progressing by comparing the cards chosen in the new reading with those from the earlier reading.

You need to spend an hour at least on these more complex spreads and record your findings for others as well as yourself, as there will be a lot of information to consider, perhaps over a day or two in your own case.

A THIRTY-THREE-CARD SPREAD FOR PAST, PRESENT, AND FUTURE

The key to the spread lies in the interconnection between past, present, and future in our life or that of the person for whom we are reading.

It is not a card formation to use with strangers, as unresolved issues both from the past and from present uncertainties can make this quite an emotive method.

Stage 1: The First Twenty-Four Cards

Use the full pack. This layout works especially well with a double pack of cards.

Shuffle and deal the cards face-down as usual, but this time with three rows of eight cards, from left to right, bottom to top, so card one is at the bottom left and facing you as you read the cards and card twenty-four is in the top right position.

ROW 1: THE PAST. CARDS ONE THROUGH EIGHT

The nearest row to you represents what has passed and is passing out of your life.

The cards nearest the beginning of the row to the left will refer to childhood and become more recent in chronological dates toward the right of the row up to the age you are now in card eight. Each card does not represent a set number of years, but any key years or events (for example, marriage) will feature as a single card in the row (maybe two if the issue is complicated or painful).

In your own reading, these key dates will be obvious; but with someone else, for example, you might get the Eight of Cups for a time the person left home. So ask if you feel a card has special significance.

This first row may contain several unresolved issues but, more positively, also those areas and people that have contributed to present success or happiness.

ROW 2: THE PRESENT. CARDS NINE THROUGH SIXTEEN

The middle row represents present influences and should also be read left to right. In the present will reside current relationships and any questions, home and work influences, personal goals, and recent achievements. This row tends to contain more consciously acknowledged factors, since unconscious influences from parents, teachers, and lost loves tend to be buried in the previous past line (one through eight).

ROW 3: THE FUTURE YET TO BE MADE. CARDS SEVENTEEN THROUGH TWENTY-FOUR

The top row looks not at a set future but at potential paths to be followed, opportunities and challenges that lie just over the horizon, and indications of the success of action or inaction. The immediate future will be to the left of the row and the more distant future to the right (up to five years ahead).

One option is to work with the twenty-four cards, reading them as I suggested. Read each card, one at a time, and, if in your own reading, keep talking to avoid your analytical mind kicking in; when reading for someone else, keep a dialogue going and seek the person's input about significant life steps and dreams.

After reading card twenty-four, add a twenty-fifth card, dealt face-down, from the main pack(s) above the middle card in row three. This final card will suggest the unexpected factor that will bring you future happiness and success.

Stage 2: The Eight Strategy Cards Twenty-Five through Thirty-Two

You do have the option with this layout to add the following eight strategy cards to the twenty-four past, present, and future cards (don't use the twenty-fifth card as I suggested above if you are adding these eight extra ones).

These extra cards can be of use in identifying strategies to move you or the person for whom you are reading from the present to the future in the most positive way and to avoid any potential hazards identified in past and present rows. Use these extra cards if the future row does not seem clear or you want further information about immediate strategies, especially if others are involved in your future decisions.

Read all twenty-four past, present, and future cards first.

Reshuffle what is left of the pack or packs if using two packs and deal eight more cards face-down from left to right.

Set these on top of the middle line of cards, left to right, so that each one of the new cards covers one of the present row cards (nine through seventeen).

One by one, turn over the strategy cards and each will tell you how to get from the present to the future in connection with the issue contained in the card it covers.

Reread the original future row again (cards seventeen through twenty-four) and they will now make perfect sense.

THE TREE OF LIFE

Were there only one full layout, I would recommend the Tree of Life, based on the old mystical Kabbalistic wisdom. This spread is easy to follow, uses only twelve cards, and is brilliant for both spiritual questions and for when there are a number of different questions or issues affecting the questioner's future, which although separate are all interrelated.

It is especially good for matters that will be of importance in the year ahead. Although each sphere lists colors and connections with planets, these are not essential for the reading. I have given keywords for each sphere to guide you.

Using the Tree of Life

Draw or scan losts of Tree of Life diagrams in advance and you can set the chosen cards on them for readings. Otherwise just layout the cards in the positions the spheres would be if on a table, bottom of the Tree to top. Some people color and laminate a special Tree of Life diagram for this spread.

Before beginning, from a shuffled or mixed face-down pack, pick twelve cards from anywhere in the pack (not necessarily the top cards). The Tree has the highest sphere numbered as one at the top. Begin laying cards and reading with sphere ten at the bottom and work your way up.

The Tree of Life Meanings

SPHERE TEN: Earth, Areas of Concern: Practical matters, home, family, animals, everyday life, where you are now in your life.

Keywords: I have.

SPHERE NINE: Moon, Areas of Concern: Needs, wishes, desires, dreams, feelings, under the surface.

Keywords: I desire.

SPHERE EIGHT: Mercury, Areas of Concern: Communication, creativity, logic, travel, learning, risks, truth and illusion.

Keywords: I create.

SPHERE SEVEN: Venus, Areas of Concern: Love, relationships, reconciliation, growth in every area of life, harmony.

Keywords: I share.

SPHERE SIX: Sun, Areas of Concern: Success, individuality, self-confidence, work matters, determination.

Keywords: I am.

TREE OF LIFE

Start from the bottom and work yourself upward.

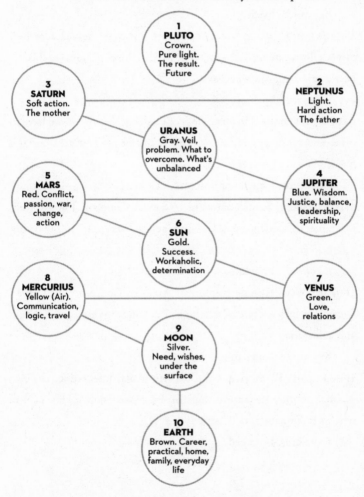

1 PLUTO
Crown.
Pure light.
The result.
Future

3 SATURN
Soft action.
The mother

2 NEPTUNUS
Light.
Hard action
The father

URANUS
Gray. Veil,
problem. What to
overcome. What's
unbalanced

5 MARS
Red. Conflict,
passion, war,
change,
action

4 JUPITER
Blue. Wisdom.
Justice, balance,
leadership,
spirituality

6 SUN
Gold.
Success.
Workaholic,
determination

8 MERCURIUS
Yellow (Air).
Communication,
logic, travel

7 VENUS
Green.
Love,
relations

9 MOON
Silver.
Need, wishes,
under the
surface

10 EARTH
Brown. Career,
practical, home,
family, everyday
life

SPHERE FIVE: Mars, Areas of Concern: Courage, action, conflict, passion for anything, victory, change.

Keywords: I strive.

SPHERE FOUR: Jupiter, Areas of concern: Justice, balance, leadership, career advancement, all permanent partnerships, personal and business, examinations, interviews.

Keywords: I achieve.

UNKNOWN SPHERE: Uranus, Areas of Concern: Problems you have to overcome, blockages, obstacles, what is just forming over the horizon for which you may have to reach out.

Keywords: I reach out in trust.

SPHERE THREE: Saturn\Saturnus, Areas of Concern: The Mother, feminine influence, gentle loving action, acceptance, nurturing others.

Keywords: I nurture.

SPHERE TWO: Neptune\Neptunus, Areas of Concern: The Father, masculine influence, decisive logical action, striving, aiming high and achieving.

Keywords: I aim high.

SPHERE ONE: Pluto, Areas of Concern: Unity, integration, the best possible results, the future that can be strived for, leaving behind what is redundant or destructive.

Keywords: I succeed.

A Real-Life Reading: Lindsey's Story

Lindsey has lost all her money, having been cheated by the man she loved, who has disappeared, having taken all their assets and sold her house from under her. She is homeless and feels, at sixty years old, that she cannot start again. Lindsey does not want revenge even if she could find him, as she knows he will have spent everything.

SPHERE TEN: The Earth; Practical matters, home, family, animals, everyday life, where you are now: Ace of Pentacles: Sorting out the practicalities, where to live. Lindsey has an old friend who lives near the south coast of England, who is working abroad for a year and does not want to rent her home out. She has already asked Lindsey to house sit and care for the animals so that would give Lindsey breathing space.

SPHERE NINE: The Moon: Needs, wishes, desires, dreams, feelings, what lies under the surface: The Moon: Most significant of all is to get the Moon card in its own sphere. Lindsey is a gifted clairvoyant and healer and ran her own teaching school online. But her partner persuaded her to give all that up to travel with him (paid for by her). Lots of her old students have contacted her to ask when she will be teaching again. Can she start again?

SPHERE EIGHT: Communication, creativity, logic, travel, learning, risks, truth and illusion: The Three of Wands: Lindsey used to be a gifted author but this was also something she had given up. She knew one of her old editors had set up a publishing company and was looking for experienced authors. Though initially this would not pay well, it would give Lindsey a way back into writing.

SPHERE SEVEN: Venus: Love, relationships, reconciliation, growth in every area of life: Five of Swords: Lindsey knew that if her old love reemerged it would be because he had spent all the money and believed he could sweet talk his way back into her life. She had heard a number of alarming things about his past since his departure, which she had closed her ears to when they were together. So for now logic has to take precedence over the practical details of her life and she has to accept she was conned (hard).

SPHERE SIX: The Sun: Success; self-confidence, individuality, work, determination: The Princess of Pentacles: A card of starting again and of learning. Lindsey had always wanted to learn hypnotherapy as a route to past-world therapies. She knew that there were grants toward training if she was prepared to do a full psychology course at a university, and there was a suitable university near her friend's home (and Lindsey said she could worry about accommodation for the final two years of study once she was on her feet again).

SPHERE FIVE: Mars: Courage, action, conflict, passion for anything, victory, change: Tower of Freedom: Lindsey knew that because of the debts run up by her ex-partner on her credit cards, the best course was to go bankrupt since she had no hope of paying and the constant calls from creditors were making her ill. Hard though it was, it was the only way she could be free.

SPHERE FOUR: Jupiter: Justice, balance, leadership, career advancement, all permanent partnerships, personal and business, examinations, interviews: Judgment: Yes, she had been foolish, but when we think we have found our twin soul, common sense can fly out of the window; her lover had promised, when his assets tied up abroad were freed, they would be rich and he would pay her back and more. So now Lindsey had to embrace the rebirth aspect of this card and accept that if his creditors found her ex-husband, then at least he would face some consequences for his actions.

UNKNOWN SPHERE: Uranus: Problems you have to overcome, blockages, obstacles, what is just forming over the horizon that you may have to reach out for: Two of Swords: These were Lindsey's fears, her sense of failure, for she had worked hard all her life, but she knew she had to act, because her life was getting worse by the day and the debts spiraled. The Tower was the first step.

SPHERE THREE: Saturn\Saturnus: The Mother, feminine influence, gentle loving action, acceptance, nurturing others: The Empress: Surprisingly, her much older sister, who had not spoken to her for years, had heard of Lindsey's plight and offered her both financial help and a roof over her head. Lindsey knew she could not live with her sister, nor accept money, but the revived kinship had healed old wounds and restored her faith in humanity.

SPHERE TWO: Neptune\Neptunus, The Father, masculine influence, decisive logical action, striving, aiming high and achieving: Three of Pentacles: A lovely card of rebuilding step by step and also an assurance that, by the time her friend returned, Lindsey would have enough money to rent accommodation on the south coast, which she loved, for the final two years of her degree.

SPHERE ONE: Pluto: Unity, integration, the best possible results, the future that can be strived for: The Star: A promise that within twelve months Lindsey would see her new and slimmed-down dreams coming true. Twelve months later, Lindsey has rebuilt her online teaching school and indeed expanded it to face-to-face consultations. She is publishing again and is about to start her second year of a degree. Her friend has persuaded Lindsey to move into the annex of the house for the final two years of her degree and keep an eye on the house whenever her friend goes away.

CONCLUSION

This is the end of *A Little Bit of Tarot* and the beginning of your tarot journey. Always remember, however hard the path, our destiny lies within us and we can fulfill our dreams. We can use the tarot as a guide, as well as for encouragement that what lies over the next hill will be wonderful and exciting.

For we can make it so.

INDEX